# Knitting and Crochet for Beginners:

*2 Books in 1 to Easy Learn How to Knit & Crochet.*
*The Ultimate Guide With Step-By-Step Instructions, Patterns and Stitches.*

Vicky Mandala

# TABLE OF CONTENTS
## CROCHET FOR BEGINNERS

# TABLE OF CONTENTS

## KNITTING FOR BEGINNERS

# Crochet for beginners

*A simple beginner's guide to learn easy modern crocheting, with patterns and stitches. How to realize beautiful creations and discover amigurumi techniques.*

# Introduction

What do Eva Longoria, US President James Buchanan, Debra Norville and Madonna have in common? Crochet. Believe it. Debra Norville even has her own yarn line. These are just some of the people who have been hooked on crochet (pun intended).

Crochet is one of the oldest forms of craft. It has also been one of the main methods in creating clothing for thousands of years. Crochet is basically creating fabric and clothing from yarn and thread with a hook.

## The History of Crochet

There isn't an exact date when crochet started. It has been mentioned throughout earlier times. Experts claim that this craft has been around as early as 1500 to 1800 BC. Basing on the hand technique of basic crochet, it is presumed to have originated in the Middle East. Some claim that crochet actually originated in China and only spread to its neighboring countries such as the Middle East and eventually to Europe.

Crochet became most notable when French nuns started to crate elaborate and delicate patterns. They were known to create complex lacework using very fine materials. They made table clothes used to cover the altar and adorn the church. It was said that the art of crochet was a closely guarded craft among the nuns. It became an integral part of life in the convent.

Over the years, crochet found its way to Scotland and England. From the nuns, the knowledge and skill were passed on to the upper class. Crochet circles were established among the ladies of the upper class. The work was no longer focused on delicate and complex lace but was just as elegant. During those times, the skill was limited among the upper class. The poor were not given the privilege to learn the craft.

During the Renaissance, both the upper and lower classes were practicing crochet. During this time, the ladies were using macramé, which is several fine threads knotted together. They made delicate lacework which became popular across Europe.

In the 1820s, crochet was introduced in Ireland. They used fine threads and made delicate work that imitated English lace. It became known as Irish lace. Over the years, Irish lace became very popular in Europe, especially in the Balkans.

By the early 1900s, yarns changed from fine threadlike materials to something much thicker. Hook sizes also changed in order to accommodate the thicker yarns. Patterns started even more simplified, a deviation from the complex lacework in last years. Crochet items progressed from lacework such as table covers and church adornments, into something more practical such as gloves and scarves.

## Modern Crochet

Today, crochet skills are too simple compared to how the French nuns used to make them. The craft has become widespread, but the skill levels can be compared to the level of primary school crochet. It is still considered fabulous but way below the level that crochet used to be.

Also, compared to decades ago, there are considerably fewer people who are interested in the craft. Learning the skill is no longer confined to closed groups, but fewer people are willing to try. Mass production and cheaper goods have made people less inclined to making their own socks or blankets.

However, there are still a considerable number of people who keep the skill ever evolving. There are still people who wish to learn the craft.

Today's patterns are simpler. Popular ones include baby items such as sweaters, socks, bonnets, booties and blankets. Other items include Afghans and adult wear such as scarves, socks and sweaters.

## Knitting vs. Crochet

Crochet is often confused with knitting. They are closely related but very different in ways, too.

## Common elements:

The following are common elements between knitting and crochet, which often creates the confusion between the 2 crafts:

- Both knitting and crochet use yarns and other similar fibers.
- Both crafts create similar items such as sweaters, blankets, Afghans, wraps, hats, socks, mittens, shawls, and scarves, among others.
- Both base projects on patterns that use abbreviations. Some abbreviations are even the same in knitting and crochet.
- Skill sets are similar between the two, which includes good hand-eye coordination, affinity for fiber, a good

eye for design and color and patience to see a project through.

## Differences:

The main difference is on the supplies used. Knitting can use knitting needles, knitting looms and knitting machines. Crochet uses only one for all projects- a single crochet hook. The hook sizes determine how big the stitches turn out to be. Crochet has always been made by hand. The movements in crochet are so elaborate that it has yet to be replicated by a machine.

Another difference is the structure of the fabric made. While both crafts involve manipulating loops, how the loops are built differs. In knitting, the loops are built on top each other. Several loops are active at the same time, held in place on the knitting needle. One dropped stitch can cause an entire column of stitches to drop. In crochet, only a few loops are active at the same time. The stitches also build on top of each other, but the active loop is only limited to a single pot. This way, a dropped stitch will not cause a bunch of stitches to unravel.

# Chapter 1: Types of Crochet

## Amigurumi Crochet

This type of crochet is said to have originated from Japan. People would use this type of crochet when making toys that would be stuffed using this crochet. Ami means knitting or yarn that has been crocheted while amigurumi means a doll that has been stuffed. This type of crochet is therefore used when one is making these stuffed dolls through the use of heavy yarn. One can also make fan items and the large novelty cushions as well as the homewares.

# Aran Crochet

This is a type of crochet that is normally ribbed and also one that is cabled. It is a traditional type of crochet which is made through interlocking cables. Through this type of crocheting, one can make sweaters and chunky beanies as well as scarves. This type of crocheting is said to produce very strong items as a result of the interlocking of the cables. This is the reason why people use it to make items that would need to be worn for longer periods of time. They can also be used to make blankets and aphgans as well as jackets and coats and also scarves.

# Bavarian Crochet

This is a type of crochet which is said to work just like the granny squares, which were traditionally made. It is used when one wants to make very thick items and also when they want to blend in different colors when making them. This type of crochet is said to allow people to be able to blend in different colors without experiencing any challenges. They are able to do this by working on each part on its own. This helps them to be able to blend them together, which makes them come up with a very fancy item. The granny squares make it very appealing since one can even use squares of different colors. One can make blankets and shawls through the use of Bavarian crochet.

# Bosnian Crochet

Bosnian crochet is used when one wants to make a dense and knit like materials through the use of a crochet slip sew up. One has to, however, stitch different parts of a stitch on the current row. One has to ensure that the stitches are different in each row. They are able to achieve this through the use of the Bosnian crochet hooks, which are said to produce very good crochets. One can still work with the normal hooks; even the Bosnian hooks give better crochets than the other hooks.

This type of crochet is not very popular. This is because one would think that it is normal knitting when you look at the crochet. It is easy to work with it since the style used is easy to learn. People use it when one is making the scarves and beanies, as well as when crocheting items that do not require much time to be crocheted.

# Bullion Crochet

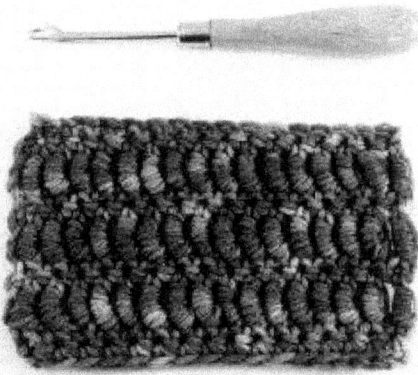

This is a type of crochet that requires one to use a lot of time when making them. One uses many wraps of the yarn, which have to be put around a hook that is very long. By doing this, one is able to come up with a very unique stitch. This type of crochet is used when one needs to make the motifs and not when making crochets that require one to use the fabrics.

It takes a lot of time to produce the item you are making using this type of crochet since one has to be very keen when coming up with the patterns. The final product is normally very firm and thick, as well as stiff. A crocheter uses a method to make items that are meant to be long-lasting. One can make mats and stiff materials when they use this type of crocheting. This helps them to be able to come up with materials that are very unique and firm, so they can be used for a very long time without them wearing out.

# Broomstick Crochet

This type of crochet is also called jiffy lace. It is normally made through the use of traditional crochet hooks. One form makes some stitches all round a very long as well as wide stick that looks like that one of a broomstick. In this modern age, people are said to use the large crochet hooks as well as the thick dowel when they are making the broomstick lace nowadays. It is a skill that people need to take their time to learn in order for them to come up with a well-made crochet. It is, however, a type of crochet that is said to produce crochets that are very beautiful and unique. One can make baby shawls using this type of crochet and also throw blankets that are normally used for the purposes of decoration.

# Bruges Crochet

This is a type of crochet that is used when one wants to make Bruges laces, as the name suggests. One first creates ribbons meant for the crochet, which are sewed together in order for them to form the desired lace pattern. They are said to form very beautiful patterns that are also unique. This is because they are neatly sewed together. One can use different colors when making these patterns, which makes them even more beautiful. This type of crochet is used for making table mats and shawls as well as embellishments that are used for clothing.

# Clothesline Crochet

This is a type of crochet which is said to utilize the stitches that were used traditionally. One uses a very thick yarn when making items using this type of crochet. They work on a rope that has to be very thick since when making mats, one requires something that will be so strong, and which will be easy to style as well as shape. This type of crocheting is mostly used when one is making mats and baskets or anything that is required to be strong. One needs to have skills on how to make items using this type of crochet since they need to make first make the item they need to make on the ground before they can crochet it. This type of crochet is used in the making of mats and baskets as well as wall hangings.

# Clones Lace Crochet

This type of crochet was said to be easy to make in the past and was very popular among people who love crocheting. It resembled the Irish lace, which was made because it was so easy to make. Clones knots are made, which makes as they are normally part of the crocheting process. One needs to learn this skill in order for them to ensure that they know how to make items using it. This type of crochet is used when one is making delicate dresses that require one to be very keen.

# Cro-hook Crochet

With this type of crochet, one is required to use a hook that is double-sided in order for them to be able to achieve crochets that are double-sided. The crocheter is expected to work on an item from both sides. He or she can work from either side of the item, which enables them to come up with a very unique pattern. It is important for a crocheter to be able to learn this style before using it to male items in order for them to get good out of the outcome from it. One can make baby clothes and scarves as well as washcloths through this type of crocheting.

# Filet Crochet

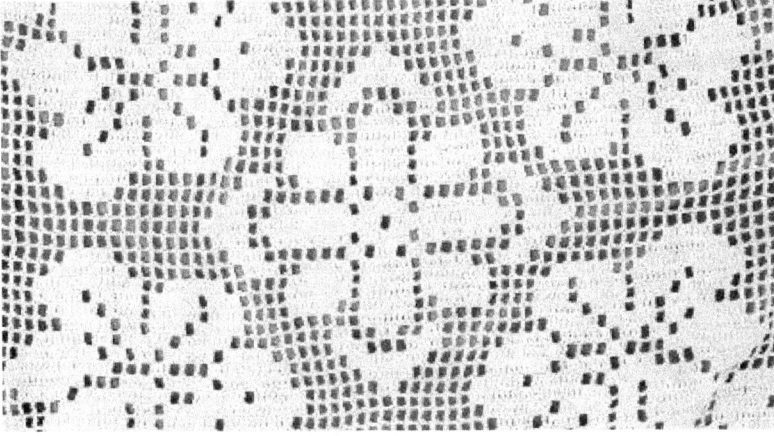

This crochet is a style that is achieved through the use of chains as well as double crochets. One achieves a crochet that has a pattern that is grid-like, which can be filled or left without filling. The space that is left is used in the creation of desired pictures which have to be included in the design. It creates patterns that are so unique and are neatly embedded within the crochet. This is something that is so unique about this type of crochet. All the squares that are left empty when crocheting may be filled with pictures of one desire. This type of crocheting is used when one is making the baby blankets, handbags, jackets, and kimonos, as well as when they are making cushions.

# Finger Crochet

Finger crocheting is practiced when one barely uses the hook when crocheting. It is used when one is making some hand fabrics. During this type of crocheting, one will mostly use their hands to crochet. The patterns are fixed together to come up with one complete item. When one is making fabrics using this type of crochet, one cannot do it too fast. They will spend a lot of time crocheting, which may make them make very few items for a very long period of time. One can only make some string bags and small scarves which do not require much time when making them.

# Freeform Crochet

When making this type of crochet, one does not create any pattern on the item. It is crocheting that very artistic in nature and also very organic. Crocheter does not follow any plan, so one can come up with any kind of design that they would want. There are, however, people who do not like this type of crochet since they cannot do it without any kind of plan. They need to follow some instructions in order for them to be able to make their desired patterns. One can make art pieces using this type of crochet. They can design anything that they desire to design.

# Hairpin Crochet

This is a type of crochet which is said to work just like the broomstick crochet even though in the past, people used crochet hooks. Pieces being crocheted were held together through the use of metals that were then. One is able to get very beautiful and unique crochets which are well finished. They are used when one is making shawls and wraps as well as scarves.

# Micro Crochet

Micro crochet is used by the modern woman to make crochets. They make use of threads that are very fine and crochet hooks that are also very fine. A crocheter has to make sure that they are very careful when using the hooks in order to ensure that they use them in the right way in order for them to make the best types of crochets. They are used when one is making the talisman and embellishments as well as when making teeny tiny things.

# Overly Crochet

Overly crochet is used when one wants to achieve an item that has stitches on top of the item, which enables them to be able to get a pattern that is raised. One can use more than one color when crocheting, which will enable them to be able to achieve unique and beautiful patterns. They can also make different designs using this type of crochet. One can use this type of crochet when making potholders as well as wall hangings as well as handbags.

# Pineapple Crochet

When making items using this type of crochet, one does not follow any given pattern. This is because one can use just one general stitch, which they use to shape their desired patterns. One can use the pineapple when making these patterns. They use it to make scarves and shawls as well as wraps. This type of crochet is not complicated since anyone can learn it and be able to crochet items into their desired designs.

# Chapter 2: Crocheting Supplies: Tools and Materials

Here are the basic materials for starting up a crochet project:

- Yarn
- Crochet hook
- Scissors
- Darning needle
- Tape measure
- Hook organizer
- stitch markers
- Row counter
- Stitch patterns
- Crochet material organizer

The materials help in one way or another in making crochet. However, for beginners, one can use the basic ones.

# Yarn

Yarn is a thread used in sewing or knitting any form of material. This is the backbone of crochet. It is the only material that comes out of the final product as it carries everything from designing to the conclusion. For beginners, it is advised to use a medium weight yarn as it is easy to crawl it with the hooks.

There are different types of yarns according to your preference and it is better to understand them before buying. The common material is polyester and wool. There is also nylon, acrylic, rayon and viscose which can be the best choice according to one's preference.

Here are the types of yarns:

- Natural fibers
- Synthetic fibers
- Eco-friendly fibers

Natural Fibers

These are yarns made from natural materials.

Cotton

This is a material harvested from cotton plants a process is used to preserve them to last longer.

Silk

This is form of material made from the larvae of silkworm and is mostly incorporated with other fibers to create a neat and long-lasting yarn.

Cashmere

Just from its name, you can see it is drawn from a cashmere goat and is known for being soft and warm at the same time.

Linen

This is harvested from a flash plant and is commonly used for light garments.

Wool

This is so common in clothes and yarn and it is a perfect material for heavy yarns.

Synthetic Fibers

As stated above, this is the commonly preferred materials for yarn and is among the selling materials in the world. This includes nylon, polyester, acrylic, rayon, and viscose.

Eco-friendly fibers

Organic Cotton

This is cotton made from cotton plants and is not treated with chemicals.

Bamboo

Bamboo has always created many products for different uses and its silk is harvested as it makes a perfect yarn because of its strength.

Those are just a sample of the commonly used yarns which are formed from different fibers for different types of crochets according to users' need.

# Hooks

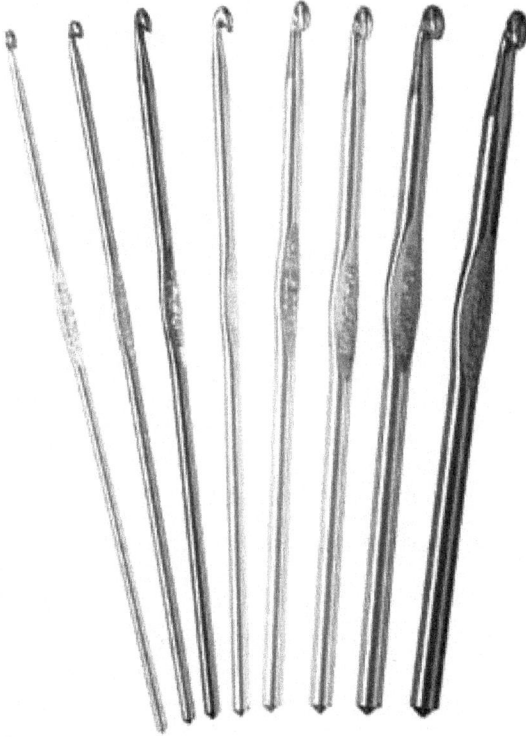

This is primarily the needles used to hook up and do stitching on yarn to form crochet. The hook drives the yarn on each one in a back and forth manner to form beautiful crochet. Sometimes, it is used concurrently with needles when a misstep is made on crochet.

Hooks come in different sizes and it is better to choose a perfect one depending on the yarns' sizes and design. It is advisable to always consider all these before starting up for some hooks may not perfectly fit your desired project.

# Scissors

This is a tool commonly used in homesteads for homemade clothes or trimming of oversized curtains and towels. It is also known for being used by tailors for cutting their materials and another trimming of textile. Scissors on crochet are also paramount.

Just like the hooks, the scissors have its types and different functions on a craft or any material using yarn and hooks. The basic one is the general craft scissors which can be found locally and easily. It is okay to use the general craft scissors on different fibers because it does not leave sharp edges and cuts in a zigzag manner just like the pinking shears. Here, the type of scissor does matter when the crochet is in the completion stage as it helps cut it into nice pieces without producing threads and tears inappropriately.

When buying them online, make sure you check their specifications, as others might not be suitable for your project. The recommended scissors are standard, snips, embroidery scissors, and lastly the dressmaker. Embroidery scissors could be perfect for this case because it helps cut the exact yarn being used without tampering with the rest of the project.

# Darning Needle

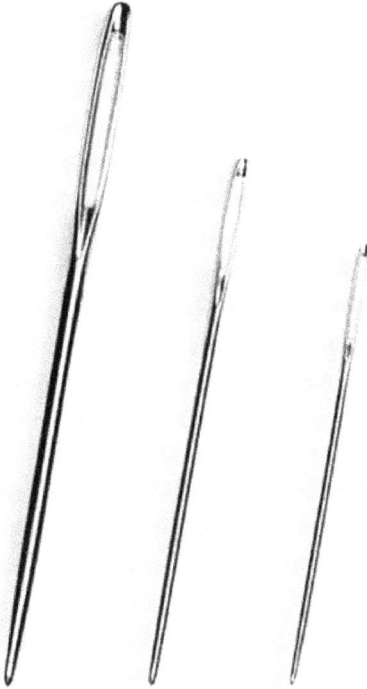

As the name suggests, it is a form of a needle with a bigger hole than the normal needle where the yarn passes through. The sharp end is a little blunt compared to a sewing needle and helps in making a perfect end on crochet. The darning needle is used to fix the end of each crochet to enable it to stay stable when in use. This is similar to sewing where you tie a knot in the end of the material, but for crochet, the darning needle is used to make the knot, which will keep the whole crochet intact and in perfect shape.

There is no big problem when choosing a darning needle as one can compare with the size of the yarn and its hole to see if it perfectly fits. The one with a larger hole can accommodate every kind of yarn and there should not be any problem whatsoever.

# Stitch Markers

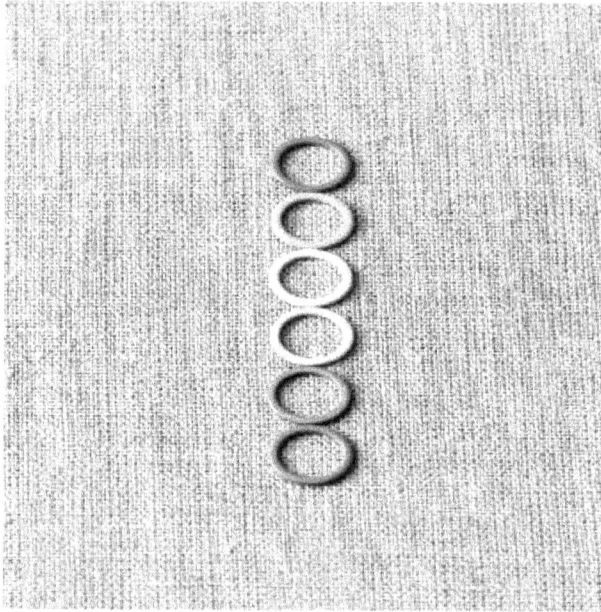

These are clips used to mark areas of interest in crochet. There are different designs of crochets and when you have a slightly complex craft; it is always advisable for one to have a stitch marker. For beginners, it is always complicated to make crochets with corners or even rounded by following the pattern. This means the stitch markers are perfect for making areas where it forms patterns unless one is a professional.

Stitch makers have crafted clips that help indicate or put marks on a design to help a beginner or a craftsman to have a perfect and uniformed crotchet.

Any size and type of stitch markers can be used on any piece and type of yarn, as it does not favor the material. The maker can be found in local stores and most people prefer them depending on the sizes of their hands, or how perfectly they can hold them.

# Tape measure

Some of you could be wondering why almost everything that is used by tailors is being used to craft crochet, and the answer is yes, it needs to be totally perfect. Tailors are always seen with tape measures and to make crochet, you might want to get one too, especially for a beginner. The tape measure is simply for measuring and making the right adjustments when following a designed pattern.

This is a necessary tool when there is clipping using stitch markers as it will help to create uniform patterns and with minimal or no blundering.

However, for crochet flowers, this might not be necessary as they are very simple and can be modified easily, but it is advisable for big projects and to avoid disappointments at the end of it with different and unorganized sizes.

Tape measures also come in different sizes and types and other specifications depending on the country you are located in. For a clear understanding, make sure you get a tape measure that supports your form of measurements. For instance, America's measurement is different from Russia's and the United Kingdom. To make perfect measurements, beware of the measurements placed as some may be misleading or have different calculations depending on their form of measurements.

## Stitch Patterns

These are the format you at achieving at the end of your projects. This can also be found in tutorials of some craft enthusiasts who have knitted samples of crochets and might be a good chance to get out of your comfort zone and learn some styles or even create some at the end of the day.

For a specific stitch pattern, one can learn their way through and come up with perfect crochet by just following the simple rules. Listed below are some of the common stitch patterns for beginners and can be useful for your first project.

# i. Twist headband

These are perfect headbands one can make in one day for beginners. The twist headband can be put on the head and is perfect for the ladies to help hold their hair just like a clip. Unlike Marvin, it only covers a quarter of the hair and is comfortable and perfect for the winter season. This can be a good project for beginners.

## ii. Marion's Cozy Mug Warmer

Crochets are not only for wearing but for beauty; it is a craft and can be used in many forms. As the name suggests, this is a cover for a mug and is good for cold seasons. This is a unique design and also simple for beginners who are looking forward to creating beautiful designs.

## iii. Snowflake Patterns

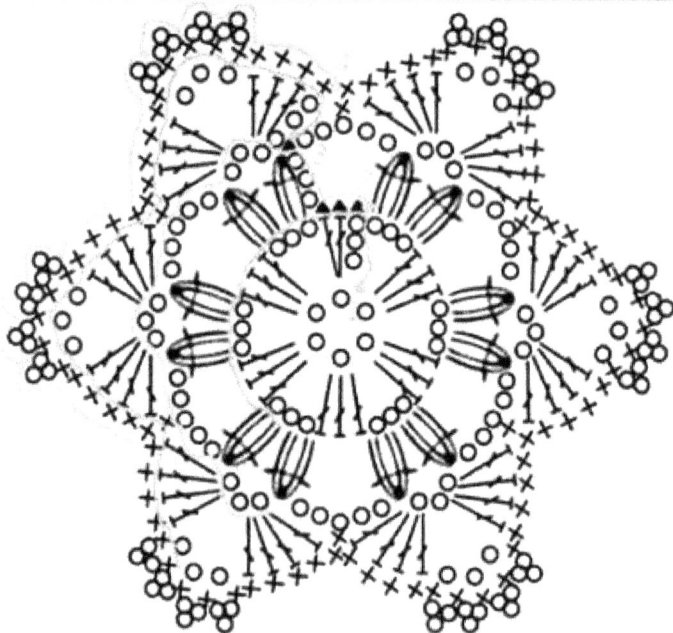

Nothing is as perfect as a snowflake and its design is even mind-blowing. It may look like a tiny piece but when done, it is perfect crochet that can be made with easy steps. They can be used to beautify the house or even create designs in clothes.

# iv. Jingle Bell stocking

When you hear the word jingle bell, what rings in the mind is not a bell but Christmas, yes, the stockings are made using yarn and it makes a good crochet for a beginners' project. They are made to look like the Christmas attire for Santa Claus and can be spiced up by using red and white color.

With these stitch patterns, one can create a lovely design for beauty purposes or even gifting a loved one. A beginner should always keep an eye on the prize, which is the ultimate pattern that will be a result of the design.

# Hook Organizer

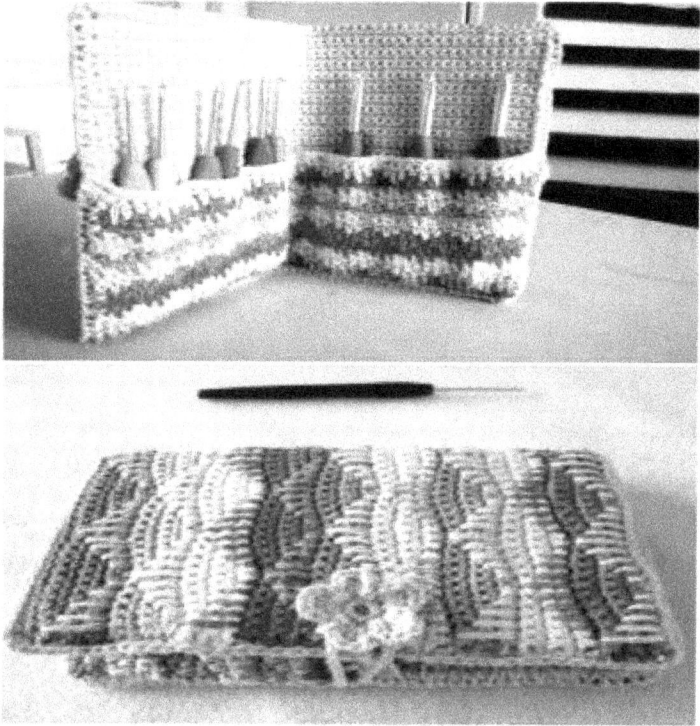

After making the first and second pattern, you get to know the stitch patterns and designs that can work for you as you continue to be creative and innovative. The hook organizer resembles a toolbox for a car which is always referred to as Do It Yourself and can work on your car anytime, anywhere. For the crochet, this is almost similar as it carries your essential materials for the work.

After finishing the work, the hook organizer helps keep all the materials used as it has pocket-like spaces for placing hooks, tape measure, darning needles, yarn and other combinations of crochet tools. One can make any design that can hold the materials with ease and keep them in order. Instead of buying a toolbox for such materials, make one to be among the projects and you will be shocked at how you continue to perfect your craft.

# Chapter 3: Crochet Terminology

You now know the basics of crocheting, and you're ready to move on to something a little more complicated. Before you do though, you'll need to learn the numerous abbreviations that are used in these patterns so that you can read them correctly. These terms will be used in this for the patterns as well, making sure that you get used to them to help you move forward.

The first thing to know is that the UK and the US do label stitches differently, so you'll need to know where it comes from if you want to understand your patterns properly. You'll find an easy conversion chart below.

| UK | | US | |
|---|---|---|---|
| Chain | Ch | Chain | Ch |
| Slip stitch | Ss | Slip stitch | Ss |
| Double crochet | Dc | Single crochet | SC |
| Half treble | Htc | Half double | Hdc |
| Treble | Tr | Double | Dc |
| Double treble | Dtr | Treble | Tr |

| Triple treble | Ttr | Double treble | Dtr |
| --- | --- | --- | --- |

## Skip a Stitch:

This means that you'll miss your following stitch. You will continue with the following one after the stitch that you've skipped.

## Dc2tog:

This is an abbreviation that means you need to put two double crochet stitches together to form one stitch. To do this, you'll need to put your hook into the following stitch, and then perform yr (yarn over), and then draw it completely through. Don't finish the dc (double cross) stitch. The hook will then need to be put into the following stitch, yr, and then pulled completely through it. This will put three loops on your hook when done correctly, and then yr to pull them together.

## Foundation Chain:

A foundation chain will be your base chain and you'll add stitches on top of it. This is what you'll work all of your following stitches back into.

## Foundation Row:

This is a little different than a foundation chain, as it's the row that you're working into the foundation chain.

## Turning Chain:

You've already learned how to turn a chain, and turning chain refers to the stitches that you're using as extras to work with at the beginning to create the new row. It'll bring you up to the proper height to start the following row. Different stitches can require different numbers of these stitches to work properly.

## Dc3tog:

This is commonly called the cluster stitch. This is where you work three of your dc stitches into one, and you'll be working with the three stitches in a row, but it'll result in four loops being on your hook. Yr., drawing it through all four

Acrylic: This is a synthetic yarn, which is why it is more affordable.

Black Loop Only: This is where you'll focus only on the back loops that you are making.

Back Loop SC (Single Crochet): This is another variation of a SC stitch, which will focus on just the back loops when making it.

Color Flashing: This is seen in many patterns, and it's an effect that happens if you're using a variated yarn. You'll have unintentional patterns show up in your work, which will create unique patterns.

Coned Yarn: This is a yarn that has been wound onto a holder that is cone shaped, and it's often easier to work with as you move on to more complex patterns.

Floats: When crocheting, there are some unused pieces of yarn, or rather strands that will be carried onto the back of the project.

Frog: This is used as a verb in crocheting, such as "to frog". It is to rip out your stitches. This will add decorative or functional pieces. This can be used for when you're adding buttons.

Freeform Crochet: This is where you aren't crocheting from a pattern, and this is great when you're practicing your stitches. You explore the craft, and you'll usually end up with a unique pattern.

Granny Square: This is a crochet pattern that is just made of a simple ring of chain stitches, and then you build on it outward. They are often put together to make a blanket.

Inelastic: When you're working with an inelastic yarn it won't recover its original shape quickly if at all after you've stretched it.

Kitchen Cotton: When you're looking for a yarn that's easy to use and useful in projects, you'll want to find kitchen cotton. You can use it for placemats, potholders, and even dishcloths.

Pjoning: Once you know how to use ss (slip stitch) easily, you'll be able to move on to a pjoning, which is where you use it to create different, unique fabrics.

Plarn: You'll find this when you're shopping for yarn, as it's a plastic yarn. It's often recycled, where bags and other plastic items were cut up and repurposed.

Place Maker: You'll want to use these when you have to stop a project, and it's where you mark it in a way that you can remove so that you don't lose your stitch. Many people will use safety pins that can easily be taken out.

Protein Fiber: This is a fiber made from protein, but it's not something a beginner should be using.

Scrapghan: This is where you make an afghan, which can be put together through granny squares or granny triangles, but you use your yarn Scraps to make it. This will often have a large variety of colors and yarn types.

Shell Stitch: You'll learn this as one of your last stitches, and it's where you've looped multiple stitches into a single one.

Tapestry Needle: This is a sewing needle that is often used in embroidery.

Variated Yarn: This is a yarn that has a variety of colors, allowing for unintentional patterns of color to appear in your pattern.

Self-Striping Yarn: This is a type of variated yarn, and it has two or more colors in it. It usually does not change colors quickly, so you'll have long stretches of each color. You can get some variegated thread that has a shorter stretch of each color.

Work Even: This is your goal with most patterns, especially as a beginner. You'll want to continue in the same stitch pattern. You do not want to increase or decrease.

Worsted Weight Yarn: You'll find this in many simple patterns, and it just means a medium weight.

Yarn Cake: This is a method that you use to wind yarn.

Abbreviations:

| Beg- beginning | Hdc- half double crochet | Sp(s) – space(s) |
|---|---|---|
| Bg- block | Htr – half treble crochet | St(s)- stitch(es) |
| Cc- contrst color | Inc- increase | Tog- together |
| Ch- chain | Rep- repeat | Tr—treble crochet |
| Dc- double crochet | Rnd- round | Tr tr- treble treble crochet |
| Dec- decrease | SC- single crochet | Ws- wrong side |

| Dtr- double treble crochet | Si st- slip stitch | Yo- yarn over |
|---|---|---|
| [ ] = work instructions within the brackets. Do this as directed | | |
| ( ) = work within the parentheses as the instructions direct you. It'll tell you how much to do so | | |
| *= repeat what instructions followed the single astrix. Follow the directions | | |
| **= repeat the instructions that followed the double asterisks, as directed and so on | | |

Refer to the chart above if you get lost trying to understand abbreviations in patterns and projects. Eventually, you will memorize them, but a chart is always helpful when you're just starting. For an added benefit, you'll find a symbols chart below.

| symbols | US crochet term | British crochet term |
|---|---|---|
| ● | slip stitch | |
| ○ | chain stitch | |
| X | single crochet | double crochet |
| + | single crochet | double crochet |
| T | half double crochet | half treble crochet |
| Ŧ | double crochet | treble crochet |
| X̃ | crab stitch | |
| Ā | double crochet two together (dc2tog) | |
| V | 2-hdc into same stitch | |
| V | 2-dc into same stitch | |
| ⏀ | 3-hdc cluster (bobble) | |

# Chapter 4: Getting Started

For the left-handed crafters out there, you are well aware of how confusing it can be to follow right-handed methods and adjust them to suit your needs. Crochet patterns and instructions are made for right-handers unless otherwise mentioned.

There are so few left-handed crafters and being a minority, there are not many sources available to learn from. This is because only a small percentage of people are left-handed and most of them are men. So, when it comes to doing crafts, particularly crafts for women, instructions for left-handers are not a priority.

Most left-handed women use right-handed instructional tools and prefer to use those. They end up learning how to crochet with their right hand. This may be alright for some whereas others don't have as much coordination in their right hand to create a smooth rhythm. It is also possible to follow right-handed instructions and adjust them accordingly so that you can use your left hand to crochet. This can work but it is confusing at times and one needs to concentrate carefully.

So, if you are a lefty and you intend to take up crochet as a hobby, this guide should be very useful and hopefully make the process a lot easier for you.

## Let's Get Started

The most important thing is to get a firm and comfortable grip on your crochet hook as this will allow you to proceed to the next step. So, once you have a grip on it with your left hand, you'll need to use your right hand for holding the yarn. This is simply the opposite of what right-handers do.

You choose, as right-handers do, to hold your crochet hook using your thumb and your index finger to keep it in place, or you can simply grip it as you would a knife. Both ways are easy to get used to, so just decide which one you prefer using and learn to crochet that way.

There are, of course, several ways that you can hold your yarn as you work your stitches and that is up to you. One of the most commonly used methods is to loop the yarn using your right index finger. Keep the loose end up and then allow the thread that is attached to the yarn to lie on your palm in a cross manner. Once you have done this you can use the free end of the yarn to create a slip knot to start the crochet process.

Once you have done that, using your right hand then hold the slip knot you have made between your fingers' middle and thumb. This is the most comfortable position for this. Your yarn will be between your index finger and your thumb, so you' be able to control your tension nicely using your index finger. Controlling your tension will help you to create consistent, even stitches. It is best to master this from the beginning as it will make a huge difference to the quality of your work later on.

## What Is the Difference Between Right and Left-Handed Crafters?

Although it is confusing to change hands when crocheting, the main differences between right-handed and left-handed techniques are as follows:

You either grip your crochet hook in your right or left hand.

You'll hold the yarn in your free hand.

The direction you work in changes as a left-hander as you'll work your stitches from left to right whereas a right-hander will do the opposite.

To work the stitches in rounds, left-handers will work in a counterclockwise direction to the right. Right-handers will do the opposite and work their stitches in a clockwise direction to the left.

Crochet rounds worked by left-handers have a different appearance compared to those made by right-handers. Although some right-handed crocheters think that left-handers' rounds look odd, others actually prefer them.

Rows worked by left-handers look the same as those done by right-handers, except that the yarn has been fastened off on the other end, so that is the only difference.

Once you start, you'll have a piece of yarn that hangs down; this is your yarn tail. Always leave the tail hanging and never crochet over it. If a pattern has a right side and a wrong side of the work, your tail can be used to give you a hint. When the tail is hanging on the bottom right-hand corner, and then that makes it the right side to work on.

Each time that you do the yarning over, you will pick up the yarn in a clockwise direction. This is a good point to remember at all times.

## Working from Graphs

As a left-handed crafter, you'll find that most of the difficulties you'll have will lie in the interpretation of the patterns and graphs which you might use. Written patterns will be a challenge, whereas symbols are easier to use.

As an absolute beginner, you may not use graphs to start with. However, you are bound to come across them later on and use them. There are two different ones which you will use. The first is a graph used for color changes in your rows. These graphs make use of colored squares to represent the stitches. Hence, a red square indicates a red stitch in that row.

The second type of graph which you'll need to read is the graph used for the filet crochet technique (A). These are more complex and can be intimidating at first. The graph consists of blocks, which are filled in, and they represent three double crochet stitches which are worked into three separate stitches in the row above.

There are also open squares on the graph, and these are the mesh, consisting of double crochet and also chain stitches.

These graphs are marked with numbers representing the rows and stitches and are made for right-handed workers. Hence, as a left-hander, you'll need to just alter the graph accordingly. If you are not confident in doing so, you will still be able to use the graph as it is. However, the design will be reversed, and won't be exactly the same. This is not such a problem when it comes to basic designs and pictures but bear in mind that if there are any words on the graphs, they will appear as mirror images in the final product.

Here are some left-hander tips for reading graphs:

Left-handers should read the first row of the graph in the opposite direction, from left to right. Remember that right-hander will read it from right to left.

The stitches in filet graphs are normally different but the graphs read the same. For example: On the first row that falls on your right side is normally read from the left side onto right; this is the front side of the work done.

The first row of the right side gives you a basis of your work (front of work) will be read from left to right which means the work is okay while the wrong side (back of work) will be read from right to left.

Generally, the common patterns can be used by everyone, whether right or left-handed. Most of them will need to be changed slightly and also reversed. You'll learn how to do this by trial and error.

A basic adjustment that one might need to make is as follows: Join the yarn in the top left-hand corner of your piece. You'll need to do the opposite of course and join the yarn you are in use of to the upper right hand and to be specific the corner. Most times you will just need to reverse instructions such as these.

There is no need to avoid using a pattern because it is not made specifically for left-handers. The more you practice, the easier it becomes until eventually adjusting your patterns will become a habit.

# A. Filet Crochet

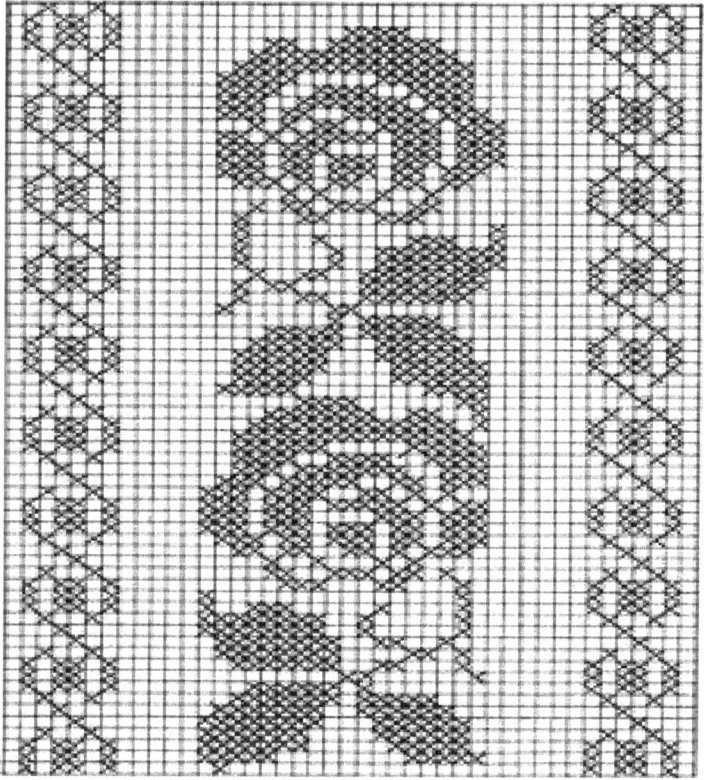

## Crochet Stitches

# How to Yarn Over (YO)

We brought this in here because you can't do any crochet work without yarning over. In fact, you are going to yarn over and as much as possible during every crochet project. Yarn over gives you extra stitches on your crochet, and you can decide on how wide you want the holes on your piece when you yarn over.

Step 1: Create a slip knot – then you append in your hook in the knot (Instructions for slip knot available below)

Step 2: use the hand that you are using to hold the hook to also keep the tail of the slip knot to prevent it from getting wider or tighter.

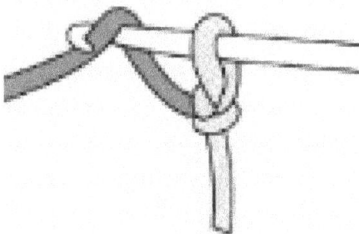

Step 3: Wrap the yarn from the back to the front (anticlockwise manner) of the hook (this is called a yarn over).

Step 4: take the yarn over the hook for the number of times instructed for the pattern.

# 1. How to Make a Slip Knot

You will start your crochet work with a slip knot, so you should be familiar with this. Do it over and over again till you master it.

Step 1: Measure about 7 inches to the end of the yarn.

Step 2: wrap it around your fingers to form a circle (a loop).

Step 3: Spread the loop formed with two of your fingers and put out the working yarn which is the longer strand into a loop with your fingers or a hook. Your loop should not be too tight.

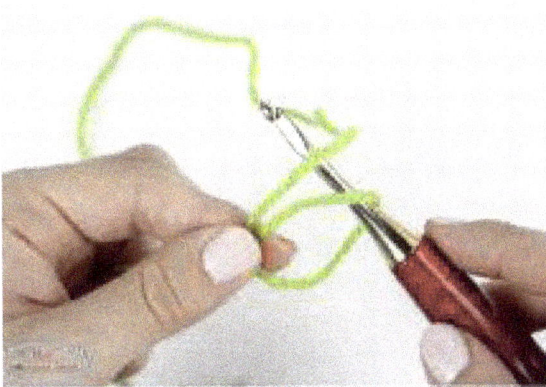

Step 4: Insert it on your hook.

## 2. How to make a Chain stitch (Ch.)

Many chain stitches, referred to as the base or foundation chain, make up the first row of a crochet piece.

Step 1: Create a slip knot – then you append in your hook in the knot.

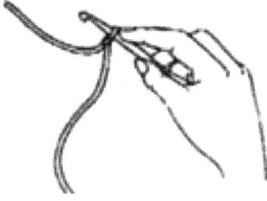

Step 2: Yarn over. After which you will then pull the yarn through the loop on the hook.

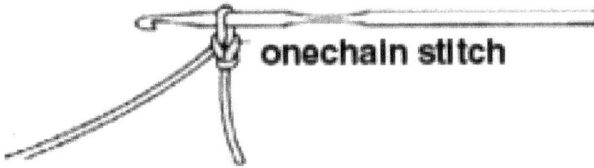

onechain stitch

Step 3: Ensure that you go through this process for as many chain stiches as required.

# 3. How to Single crochet (Sc)

In the UK, the Single crochet is usually referred to as double crochet. It is a fundamental stitch in crochet, and it provides a great way of joining crochet pieces. You can also use it as embroidery on a crochet piece.

Some crochet types basically use the single crochet as their primary stitch e.g., amigurumi.

Step 1: Make the base chain

Step 2: skip the first chain and insert your hook through the second chain.

Step 3: Yarn over (as explained above).

Step 4: pull the hook (thus pulling the yarn) through the loop. That is going to form two loops on the hook.

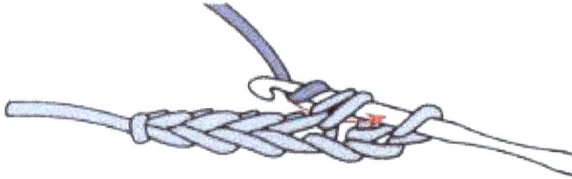

Step 5: Repeat the yarn over process while pulling the hook through the two loops to make a complete single crochet stitch.

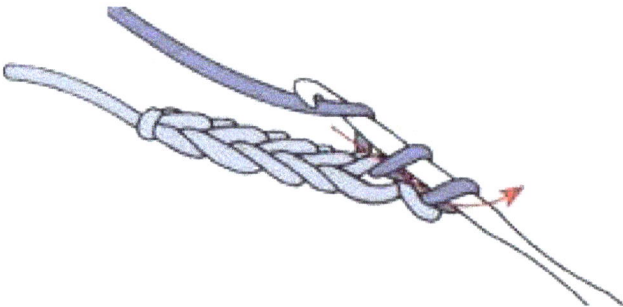

This should leave you with just one look left on the hook. You can start your following stitch from this loop.

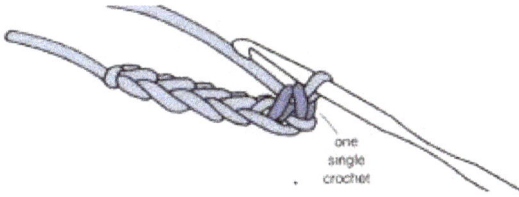

one
single
crochet

Depending on the required number of stiches for your project, you can create additional single crochet stitches to make up for them.

Moving to the following row while continuing the single crochet stitch:

Step 1: Without removing the crochet hook, turn your crochet piece from right to left (in an anticlockwise manner)

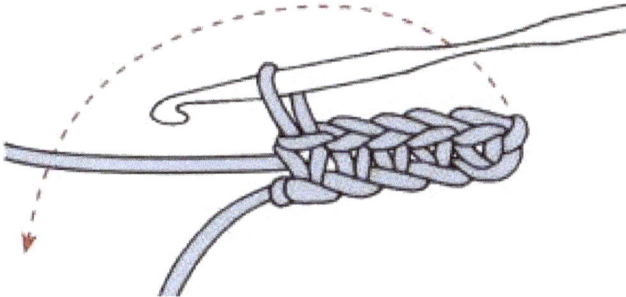

Step 2: Let the hook go into the last stitch of the first Sc row as illustrated below.

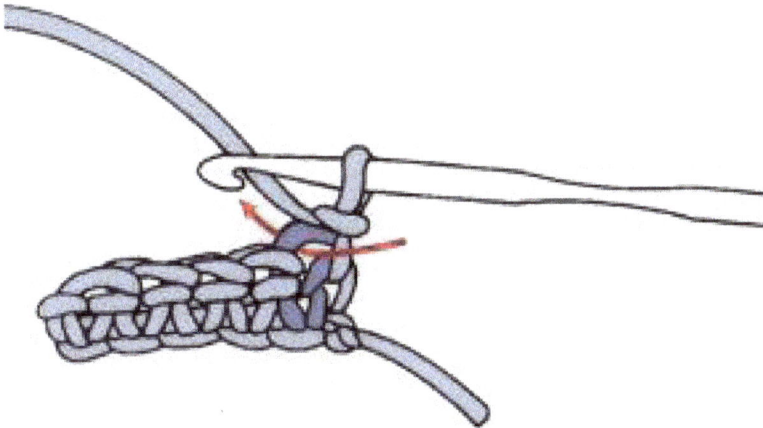

Step 3: Yarn over. Let the yarn pass through the last stitch to create two loops on the hook.

Step 4: Repeat the Yarn over again while ensuring that the yarn passes through both loops.

Ideally, you shouldn't have more than one loop left by now – that is you creating your first single crochet stitch.

# How to decrease a single crochet stitch

The abbreviation for this is sc2tog.

To decrease a single crochet stitch is simply to join it to another to make both one.

Single crochet stitches that often come out in rectangular or square forms are transformed into clothing or other stuff this way.

To get your desired shape, reduce the number of stitches that exist on the row in which the two is being joined together.

The two stitches are joined at the top, which means that after decreasing, there will be two crochet bases sharing one top.

Step 1: Using one of the pieces, let your hook go into the following stitch where the reduction of the single crochet will begin (assuming the reduction should ideally to start at the beginning of the row, then, you should make use of your first stitch)

Step 2: Create two loops by yarning over and pulling up a loop.

Step 3: Leave these 2 loops you just created and then into the following stitch, of the second single crochet, insert your hook.

Step 4: Repeat the yarn over to create a 3rd loop.

Step 5: Do a last yarn over and pull through all the 3 loops you have created on the hook to close the stitch.

# How to increase a single crochet stitch

This is easier than decreasing. You only need to work two single crochet stitches in the stitch wherever you are told to increase.

Working another stitch in the one indicated by the arrow

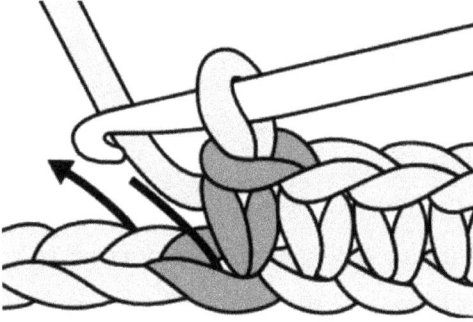

Will look like this:

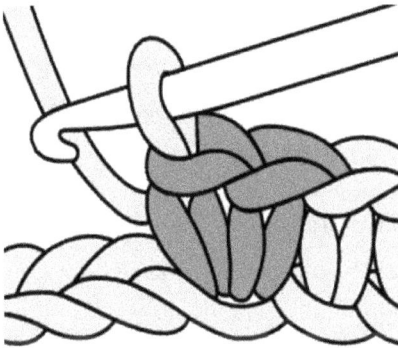

# One stitch, different styles

You can try out different styles with the single crochet stitch such as:

1. A lacier style: To create this, instead of sliding the hook under the two loops, you want to insert your hook into the front loop only of the stitch (flo) - This will create more holes in your work.

2. A closed-up style: In a case where you do not want the holes, rather you want your work closed up; you can put your hook through the bottom left. Alternate between front loop only (flo) and back loop only (blo) to get your desired style.

3. A stretchy style: So, you fancy neither the open nor the "too close" style, but you would rather have your material to 'draw,' you might want to consider inserting the hook through the back loop only (blo).

4. A standard single crochet stitch style: you get this when you insert hook through the two loops of the stitch at the same time.

# 4. How to Make a Half Double Crochet (Hdc)?

UK will call this a half-treble crochet as against the half double crochet in US terms. This type of crochet is taller than a single crochet. It is lower than a double crochet. So, when you are trying to form your own patterns, and you need something that is midway between a single crochet and a double crochet, think of an Hdc. It can be worked at the edge of a scarf or blanket to add more beauty to the crochet piece.

Step 1: make your base chain stitch for the number of Hdc stitches required for the project

Step 2: Add another chain as extra.

Step 3: While ignoring the first 2 chains as they will service as turning chains, yarn over and insert hook from front to back in the center of the third chain.

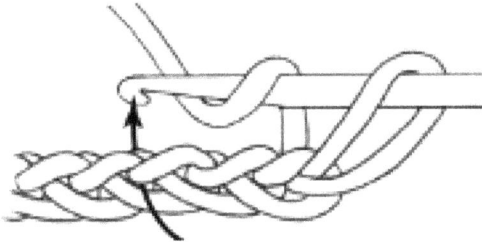

Step 4: Yarn over and draw the hook (by drawing the hook, you draw the yarn) through the chain to form three loops on the hook.

Step 5: Yarn over and draw yarn through all the three loops on the hook. There should be one loop on your hook now. That is the first half double crochet stitch.

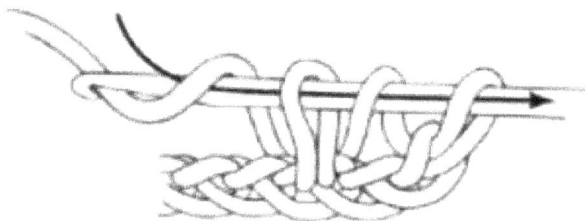

To continue with Hdc on that row

Step 6: In the center of the following chain, yarn over and insert hook.

Step 7: Again, yarn over, but this time, pull the yarn through the loop to create 3 loops on the hook.

Step 8: Yarn over and pull the yarn through all the 3 loops you created to form the second half double crochet.

Step 9: Repeat steps 6-8 to continue working Hdc on that row.

Moving on to the following row

Step 10: Turn your work. Turning chain 2

Step 11: skip the first Hdc that is below the turning chain. Use the second one instead.

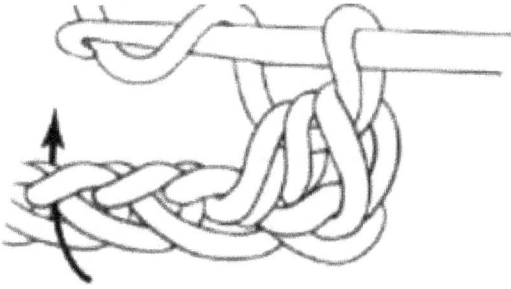

Step 12: Insert your hook from front to back and yarn over under the top two loops of the second Hdc.

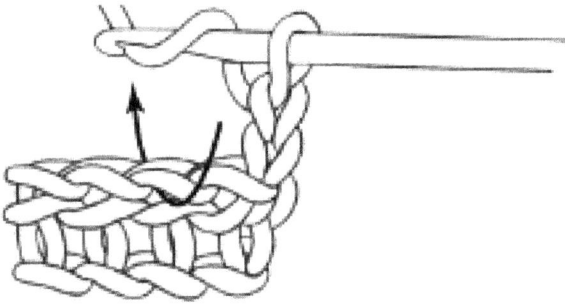

Step 13: While pulling the yarn through the stitch, yarn over just once.

Step 14: Repeat the yarn over process and pull the yarn through 3 loops on the hook to form the first half crochet stitch on that row.

Step 15: To continue working Hdc on that row, repeat steps 12-14

And just like a single crochet stitch, an instruction might call for the increase or decrease of a half double crochet. When it does, just do this:

## Half double crochet increase (hdcinc):

When you increase in half double crochet, what you are simply doing is turning one stitch into two. The pattern instruction should tell you the particular stitch to work this into.

Step 1: Make double crochet stitch (instructions above)

Step 2: Create another Double crochet stitch in the very same stitch.

## Half double crochet decrease (hdcdec):

Also, popularly referred to as half double crochet two together (hdc2tog), you can make it with these steps:

Step 1: First, you should not that what you are trying to do is to create half double crochets into not less than 2 chains without actually completing them. And to this this, you need to yarn over and insert hook into the chain to be used. Repeat the yarn over again and then pull up a loop to make 3 loops on your hook.

Step 2: Create 5 loops by repeating Step 1 for the following chains.

Step 3: Lastly, YO and then make the yarn draw through all 5 loops – after which you will then have your half double crochet decrease.

# 5. How to Make a Double Crochet Stitch

Double crochet stitches are twice the length of single crochet stitches. Crocodile stitches are typical examples of stitches you use a double crochet stich for. It is also used to decorate the edges of some crochet works.

Step 1: make the base chain to the desired length.

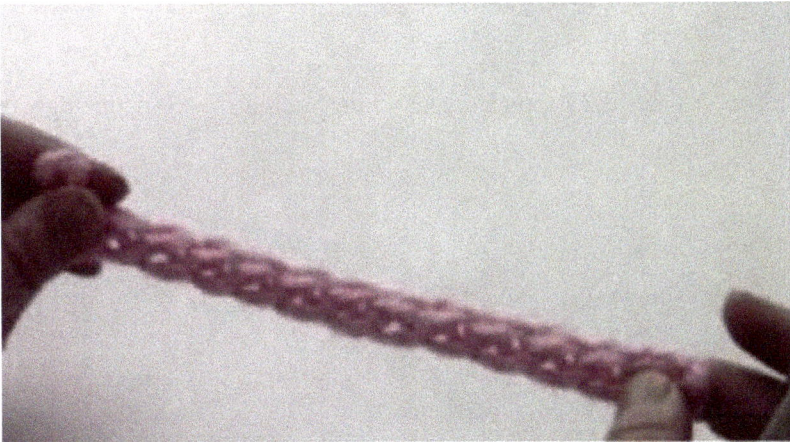

Step 2: YO while fixing your hook at the end of the 3$^{rd}$ chain from the hook.

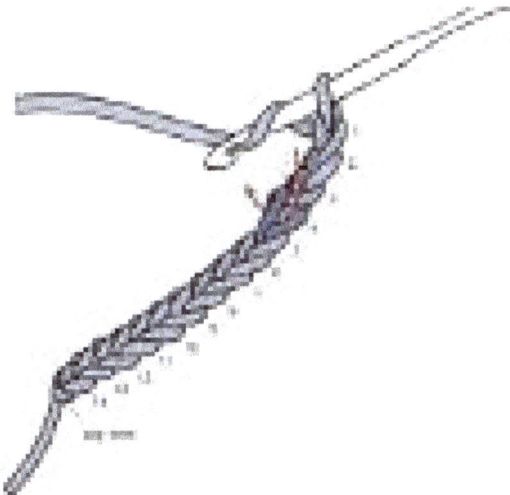

Note: The third chain is marked in red.

Step 3: Create 3 loops by YO while pulling the yarn through the third chain.

Step 4: Create 2 loops by YO while pulling the yarn through the first two loops.

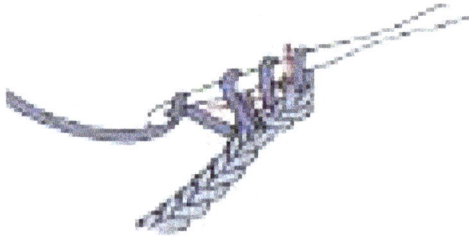

Doing as instructed and shown above will give this:

Step 5: yarn over again and pull the yarn through the two loops to complete your first double crochet stitch.

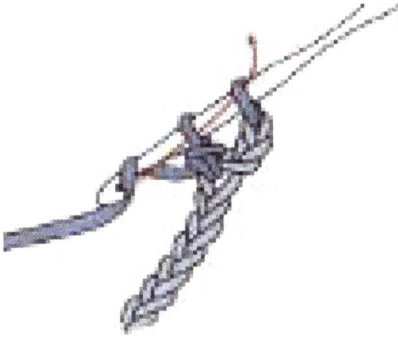

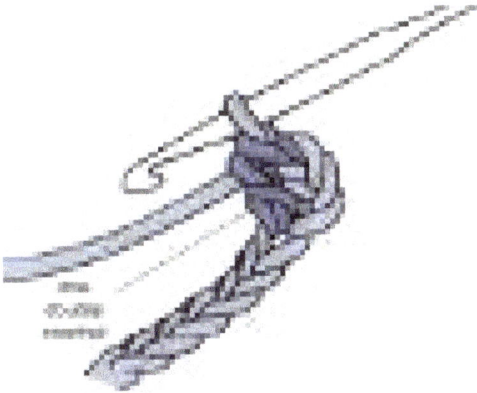

Step 6: to continue the double crochet on the following row, turn chain 3

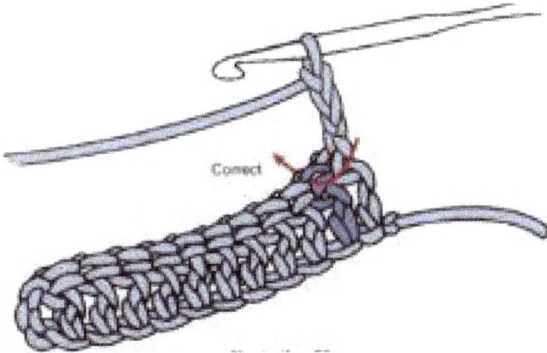

Correct

# Chapter 5: Crochet Patterns: Beginners

## DIY Scarves

Scarves are often rather straight forward when it comes to crochets, and you will find yourself making them rather quickly with the movements of that you have learned so that you do it efficiently and within a short time.

When you have finished with creating the foundation chain, you will then you will use the turning chai to create a long thin rectangle that you can keep knitting depending on how long and thus, how thick you want the scarf to be. As a beginner, this is a task that could take you a couple of hours a day, but you will be much satisfied with the outcome once you make it past the first couple of stitches.

## Granny Square

This is a prevalent crochet pattern, and you will, therefore, find great value in knowing how to go through it.

You will begin by creating the slip knot and then creating three chains. Then you start using the double crochet so that you end up with double stitches. Then once you do this, loop the two double stitches through the third chain.

Then after this, create another three of such dc clusters so that, but now you will move the dc into the foundation of the first round.

When you finish with this, repeat the first two steps, then, repeat this process, beginning with a new foundation chain from the end of one dc stitch as you create the stitching until you get to the size of the granny square that you want.

You will then use the granny square on whatever you may want, from small table mats to covers for items in the house such as sound systems and TV sets. Depending on how you have woven it, you can also use it as a cover for pillows or small furniture like stools.

This is an example of a granny square. As we see, it alternates between Sc and dc, as well as loops on chains and rows.

## Crochet Socks

Crochet socks are other easy designs that you will find it easier to so when you are a beginner.

According to Clara Parkes, the best yarns for socks are those that are elastic, meaning that they will need to stretch when you dip your foot into it, then wrap around the foot comfortably and warmly once you have worn it.

You will use your basic crochet techniques when you do this, while you will need additional experience to make more complex socks like ankle-high socks and those with frilled edges or fancy patterns.

However, if you want simple, ankle-length socks, here you will need to alternate between the single crochet and double crochet. You will alternate between these two, lapping them over each other as you move through the foundations' chains, leaving the fabric closely-knit. This is what we call the seed stitch crochet.

So, you are being with your foundation chain and then flip it over and begin to work on the turning chain, and then make the first stitch, which will work as your first double crochet in the first row. Then, start to alternate between the dc and SC, once you make your first dc, then, make the Sc after that, then the dc, Sc as you progress. Then make these stitches across the rows. When you start with a dc, you will then end the row with sc.

Once you finish, turn it over and begin working on the turning chain. But since you will have flipped over the wool, you will be working in reverse, your dc going above Sc and your Sc going above dc.

To continue creating the rows that you need, repeat the process from the moment when you made your first dc. You will repeat this process depending on how long you want the socks to be, though as a beginner, you should probably make it as short as possible as you work on your hand movements and ironing out the problems that may arise when you make a mistake.

## Crochet Seat Covers

You will find these in many homes and cars, providing the room with an antique, authentic, and comforting feel. And the thing about these is that the patterns are relatively easy to follow, with the size and design also mainly depending on how you want it. But you will want to keep it straight if you're going to create an extensive material.

Once you have done your slip knot and created your foundation chain, then make four stitches and two rows. Then, in the first round, create eight single crochet stitches then make two Sc stitches in each stitch.

In this, as with the socks, you will alternate between dc and sc. Once you create the two first rows, create another chain. Then, on the first row, the fourth chain from the hook, make dc through until the end of the row. Then, on the second chain, on the second row, make double crochet until then end. Repeat this on the third row, third chain. Once you have finished these, and then close the terms. At this point, you will have a square granny design, and you will then work from here through with additional rows and chains depending on how long you want it to be and how much you want it to cover the seat.

However, if you want to add on color and make it larger, create additional rows and chains using wool from the color that you want to infuse to the cover.

## Square Blanket

This is one other straightforward pattern that you can learn. This one will also turn out great with just one color, though you will then have to put a lot of time into it so that you can achieve the thickness and size that you want.

Using the basis of the granny square, make your foundation chain then create three more. Begin to make double crochets then, and then loop them to create double stitches. After this, then connect these two double stitches through the third chain. After this, create another three dc but with the dc going into the foundation of the first round.

Go through this step until you get to the size that you desire. Or extra thickness, you could use the technique of socks and use alternating dc and Sc to create additional loops and knots to the width that you desire.

Alternatively, you can still use this basis to create table cover, but then you will not need to make it substantial and thick as you would have with a blanket.

## Crochet Sweater for Beginners

The basis of making the sweater is starting from how you would make the granny square. Make two of such rectangles, with the size depending on who you are making it. Use dc for making the rectangle that you will make the front so that it is one solid piece with minimal gaps. You could also use this for the back or use Sc to leave a see-through back for extra aesthetics.

So, create nine chains, with two rows. Here, make an "Sc" through the second chain from the hook. Make a total of 8 sc. In the second row, stitch across the first chain, back loops only (blo). Then repeat this with the second row to row 65 or above, depending on the size to fit on waist, chest, and hips. Note that you will need the rows to be odd numbers.

Then move to the first row and in the first chain, turn it and make Sc across the band, with one running across each row, down to the number of rows that you have for the sweater and the region it fits. In the second row, loop through the third chain, turn and make double crochet across all rows. In the third row, repeat the second process. Through the fourth row through to the seventh, make the stitches on the chain lose.

Then in the 8th row, go through the third chain, turn it and make a double crochet in each dc and chain space so that you create a close-knit loop through each row until the end. In the 9th row, the third chain, make dc across all rows until the end. Use this technique for the back rectangle, but then you will use Sc and dc alternately depending on if you want the gaps or not.

## Crochet with Plastic Rings

Pure fun brings crocheting with plastic rings. A brisk job that brings results quickly. However, you should not crochet the rings individually but create coherent chains.

## Making a Crochet Ring

To start, put the normal crochet start loop on the plastic ring. The loop for the first solid ash and all subsequent hands is always pulled through the ring. Then, as usual, the two loops that are on the needle are embraced with an envelope. Repeat this until the ring is completely crocheted. Before you start work, crochet a ring completely to the sample to know how many units are needed overall. This is also dependent on wool strength.

## Connect Rings Together

The connection between two rings takes place when the first plastic ring is crocheted in half with solid hands. Now, crochet an air mesh and then the first solid mesh around the following ring.

The last ring of a row is always completely crocheted. All other half-finished crocheted rings will be completed in the second round with solid hands. In doing so, always crochet a solid piece of ash around the connecting air mesh. In the end, pull the thread through the last stitch and sew it.

The second row of rings can now also be half crocheted and connected to the rings of the first row. When crocheting the first half of the second row of rings, add the already finished first row of rings.

To do this, crochet a slit stitch into the middle stitch of the already finished ring row.

The crochet with plastic rings is particularly suitable for original placemats, small coasters, and the design of fabric bags, which receive such a special design. Of course, all these suggestions are also suitable for individual gifts.

## Filethäkeln

This crochet resembles a knotted net. One can easily distinguish between an open and closed grid background. Below is the open grid background. This is intended to make it easier for you to start, as you will usually be crocheting according to a counting pattern that is attached to the instructions.

## Crochet Flowers

These flowers are crocheted with wool for a crochet hook of strength 4 in rounds, and each of them is closed with a Kettmasche.

- ⬥ Close the chain of 6 meshes with a chain stitch to the ring.
- ⬥ 1st round: 12 fixed Sts.
- ⬥ 2nd round: in every M. 2 tr. (Replace the first trump with 3 Ch.).
- ⬥ 3rd round: Instead of the first tr. 3 Ch., Then into the first St. 1 tr., in the following M. Crochet 1 TR and 1 half TR

\* At the following 4 m. in each puncture site 1 solid St., 1 half St. and 1 St., then 2 St., in the 4. Crochet 1 TR and 1 half TR. \*

Repeat 4 times and replace the 6th sheet with 1 solid M., 1 complete half tr. and 1 tr. Cut the thread and pull it through. You can combine several individual motifs into one flower, or you can stitch together two individual motifs in different colors. Thus, simple blankets and crocheted with raffia, even carpets.

## Chapter 6: Crochet Patterns: Intermediate

# Gingerbread Man

Materials

- 4 Ply worsted weight yarn (shades of brown)
- Crochet hook
- Sequins or beads (to be used for the eyes, mouth and buttons)
- Glue

# Directions

Head

1. Round 1: Chain 3, 11 half double crochets in 3rd chain from the hook. Join with a slip stitch in the top of ch-2. (You will now have 12 stitches)

2. Round 2: Chain 1, 2 single crochets in each stitch all the way round. Join with slip stitch in first single crochet and fasten off. Leave 6" of yarn for attaching to the body. (You will now have 24 stitches)

Body and arms

1. Row 1: Chain 9, single crochet in 2nd chain from hook, single crochet into each chain all the way across, turn. (You will have 8 stitches)

2. Rows 2 to 8: Chain 1, single crochet into each stitch, all the way across and turn. Do not turn or fasten off the yarn at the end of the last row.

3. Row 9: For first arm, working at the ends of the rows, chain 1, single crochet into each of the following 3 rows. Leave the remaining rows unworked and turn.

4. Rows 10 to 11: Chain 1. Single crochet into each stitches across and turns.

5. Row 12: Chain 1, skip first stitch, 3 single crochet into the following stitch

6. Row 9: For the second arm, work in the end of rows on the opposite side of the body. Join the brown yarn with a single crochet in row 6, single crochet into each of the last 2 rows, turn. (You will have 3 stitches)

7. Rows 10 to 12: Repeat the same pattern as with that of the first arm. Sew the head to the top of the body between the arms.

Legs

1. Row 1: For first leg, with the wrong side of the body facing you, work on the opposite side of row 1. Join with a single

crochet into the first stitch, single crochet into each of the following 3 stitches leaving the remaining stitches unworked, turn. (You will now have 4 stitches)

2.  Rows 2 to 5: Chain 1, single crochet into each stitch across and turn.

3.  Row 6: Chain 1, skip first stitch, single crochet into the following stitch, 2 single crochets into the following stitch, 3 single crochets into the last stitch, slip stitch into the end of row 5, fasten off.

4.  Row 1: For second leg, with the right side of the body facing you work on the opposite side of Row 1. Join with a single crochet in the first stitch, single crochet into each of following 3 stitches, turn. (You will now have 4 stitches)

5.  Rows 2 to 6: Repeat the same pattern as with that of the first leg.

Finishing

1.  Edging for the Gingerbread Man: Using the left-over yarn from the head, join with a single crochet the first row of the arm near the head. Single crochet into each stitch, all the way round. At the end of each row work with a slip stitch as you go around to the following stitch and join with a slip stitch into the first single crochet. Fasten off the yarn.

2.  Around the outer edge of the Gingerbread Man, glue a piece of rickrack, or sew a chain stitch in a different color all the way round the edges.

3.  Glue two blue beads or sequins 1/8" apart for the eyes over top of round 1 on the head. Glue three red beads or

sequins over bottom of round 1 on the head for the mouth. Glue three green beads or sequins to the front of the body as buttons.

Crochet Holiday Pinecones

Materials

- Cotton yarn
- Crochet hook 5.5 mm
- Tapestry needle

Directions

1. Start off the pines by making a magic loop. The pinecones will be made in rounds. Round 1: 6 single crochets into the ring and pull closed. Round 2: Make 2 single crochet in each single crochet all the way round (You will now have 12 single crochets). Round 3: * single crochet into the following single crochet * repeat from * all the way round (You will now have 18 single crochets).

2. Round 4: * single crochet into the following two single crochet, increase into the following * repeat pattern * all the way round (You will now have 24 single crochets). Round 5: * single crochet into the following three single crochet, increase into the following * repeat pattern * all the way round (You will now have 30 single crochets).

3. Round 6 a: In the front loops only, *slip stitch and chain 3 into one stitch, double crochet into following, slip stitch into the following - 3 stitches* repeat pattern * all the way round, chain 1 (You will now have 10 "petals" plus chain 1). Round 6 b: In the back loops of round 5, *single crochet into the following 8, decrease once* repeat pattern * all the way round, join, chain 1 (You will now have 27 single crochets). Round 7: Single crochet into each single crochet all the way round (You will have 27 single crochets).

4. Round 8 a: In the front loops only, *slip stitch and chain 3 into one stitch, double crochet into the following, slip stitch into the following - 3 stitches* repeat pattern * all the way round, chain 1 (You will now have 9 "petals" plus chain 1). Round 8 b: In the back loops of round 7, *single crochet into the following 7, decrease once* repeat the pattern * all the way round, join, chain 1 (You will now have 24 single crochets). Round 9: Single crochet into each single crochet all the way round (You will now have 24 single crochets).

5. Round 10 a: In the front loops only, *slip stitch and chain 3 in one stitch, double crochet into following, slip stitch into following - 3 stitches* repeat the pattern * all the way round, chain 1 (You will now have 8 "petals" plus chain 1). Round 10 b: In the back loops of round 9, *single crochet into the following 6, decrease once* repeat the pattern * all the way round, join, chain 1 (You will now have 21 single crochets). Round 11: Single crochet in each single crochet all the way round (You will now have 21 single crochets).

6. Round 12 a: In the front loops only, *slip stitch and chain 3 in one stitch, double crochet into the following, slip stitch into the following - 3 stitches* repeat the pattern * all the way round, chain 1 (You will now have 7 "petals" plus chain 1). Round 12 b: In the back loops of round 11, *single crochet into the following 5, decrease once* repeat the pattern * all the way round, join, chain 1 (You will now have 18 single crochets). Round 13: Single crochet into each single crochet all the way round (You will now have 18 single crochet).

7. Round 14 a: In the front loops only, *slip stitch and chain 3 in one stitch, double crochet into the following, slip stitch into the following - 3 stitches* repeat pattern * all the way round, chain 1 (You will now have 6 "petals" plus chain 1). Round 14 b: In the back loops of round 13, *single crochet into the following 4, decrease once* repeat the pattern * the entire round, join, chain 1 (You will now have 15 single crochets). Round 15: Single crochet into each single crochet all the way round (You will now have 15 single crochets).

8. Round 16 a: In the front loops only, *slip stitch and chain 3 in one stitch, double crochet into the following, slip stitch into the following - 3 stitches* repeat pattern * all the way round, chain 1 (You will now have 5 "petals" plus chain 1). Round 16 b: In the back loops of round 15, *single crochet into the following 3, decrease once* repeat the pattern * all the way round, join, chain 1 (You will now have 12 single crochets). Round 17: Single crochet into each single crochet all the way round (You will now have 12 single crochets).

9. Round 18 a: In the front loops only, *slip stitch and chain 3 in one stitch, double crochet into the following, slip stitch into the following - 3 stitches* repeat pattern * all the way round, chain 1 (You will now have 4 "petals" plus chain 1). Round 18 b: In the back loops of round 17, *single crochet into the following 2, decrease once* repeat the pattern * all the way round, join, chain 1 (You will now have 9 single crochets). Round 19: Single crochet into each single crochet all the way round (You will now have 9 single crochets). Round 20: In the front loops only, *slip stitch and chain 3 into one stitch, double crochet into the following, slip stitch into the following - 3 stitches* repeat the pattern * all the way round (You will now have 3 "petals"). Fasten off the yarn and thread through the loose ends.

## Chapter 7: Crochet Patterns: Advanced

## Triangle

**Materials:** Choose any yarn color and hook size comfortable for you as this is a very simple project.

**Gauge:** Use any gauge for this project.

Make 14 chain stitches.

Round 1: Single crochet in the first chain stitch from the hook and each chain stitch across. You will make a total of 13 single crochets.

Round 2: Single crochet two stitches together. Make one single crochet in each of the following 9 stitches. Single crochet two stitches together.

Make 1 chain stitch then turn.

Round 3: Do one single crochet in each stitch across the row. You will have a total of 11 single crochet stitches in the row.

Make 1 chain stitch then turn.

Round 4: Single crochet two stitches together. Make one single crochet in each of the following seven stitches Single crochet two stitches together

Make 1 chain stitch then turn.

Round 5: Make one single crochet on each stitch across the row. You'll have a total of nine single crochet stitches in the row.

Make 1 chain stitch then turn.

Round 6: Single crochet two stitches together. Make one single crochet in each of the following five stitches. Single crochet two stitches together.

Make 1 chain stitch then turn.

Round 7: Do a single crochet in each stitch across the row. You'll have a total of seven single crochet stitches in the row.

Make 1 chain stitch then turn.

Round 8: Repeat Round 7.

Round 9: Single crochet two stitches together. Make one single crochet in each of the following three stitches. Single crochet two stitches together.

Make 1 chain stitch then turn.

Round 10: Make one single crochet in each stitch across the row. You'll have a total of five single crochet stitches in the row.

Make 1 chain stitch then turn.

Round 11: Single crochet two stitches together. Make one single crochet in the following stitch Single crochet two stitches together.

Make 1 chain stitch then turn.

Round 12: Make one single crochet in each stitch across the row for a total of three single crochet stitches in the row.

Make 1 chain stitch then turn.

Round 13: Single crochet two stitches together.

Round 14: Make one chain stitch. Work a round of slip stitch all the way around the outer edge of the triangle shape, putting one extra chain stitch in corners if desired, including the one at the top of the triangle. The extra chain stitch makes the corners a bit pointier.

Weave in loose ends and break the yarn.

# Round

**Materials:**

- Your choice of yarn
- Crochet hook size H-8

**Gauge:** Use any gauge for this project.

To make flat round crochet designs, you need to begin by making two chain stitches.

Important note per round: For each new round, add one extra single crochet stitch to the number of single crochet stitches between increases (increase is done by making two single crochets in one stitch).

Round 1: Make six single crochets in the second chain stitch from the hook. Slip stitch in the first single crochet to join.

Round 2: Make one chain stitch and two single crochets in each single crochet around. Slip stitch in the first single crochet to join – making twelve single crochets.

Round 3: Do one chain stitch. Join the single crochet in the following single crochet, two single crochets in the following single crochet. Repeat this around. Slip stitch in the first single crochet to join – making eighteen single crochets.

Round 4: Make a chain stitch. Do a single crochet in each of the following two single crochets, and two single crochets in the following single crochet. Repeat this around. Slip stitch in the first single crochet to join – making twenty-four single crochets.

# Spiral Flower

**Materials:**

- ⚐ Your choice of yarn
- ⚐ Crochet hook size G-6

**Gauge:** Use any gauge for this project.

Feel free to choose any yarn color to make this very stylish design!

To make the foundation, follow these rounds:

Round 1: Make four chain stitches. Join it with a slip stitch to the first chain to form a ring.

Round 2: Do eleven chain stitches. Slip stitch in the second chain from the hook and do this for the remaining nine chains. Slip stitch into the center of the ring. Turn your work 180 degrees clockwise but do not flip. Slip stitches the center of the ring.

Round 3: Work in back loops only. Single crochet into the first stitch, then make a half double crochet on the second stitch. Half double crochet into the third stitch, double crochet into the fourth stitch, double crochet into the fifth stitch. Do a turning chain into the sixth stitch; make another two on the seventh stitch, and another on the eight. Double turn chain into the ninth stitch then another on the tenth

Round 4: Make two chain stitches and turn your work.

Round 5: Work in back loops only. Slip stitch into each of the following twelve stitches. Slip stitch again into the center of the ring.

To make the petals, follow these rounds:

Round 1: Make a chain stitch and turn your work.

Round 2: Work on the front loops of the foundation, single crochet into the first stitch. Half double crochet into the second stitch. Do the same for the third. Make two double crochets into the fourth stitch. Double crochet into the fifth stitch and make a turning chain into the sixth stitch. Make two turning chains into the seventh stitch, and one of the eight. Now, do a double turn chain into the ninth and tenth stitch. After this, you should have two stitches remaining.

Round 3: Make two chain stitches and turn your work.

Round 4: Work in back loops. Slip stitch into each of the following twelve stitches. Slips stitch the center of the ring.

Round 5: Repeat Round 1-4 until you make 10 petals.

Weave in your ends.

# Octagon

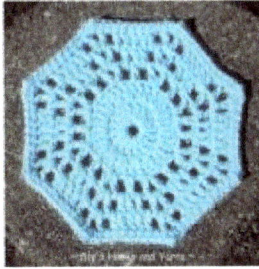

**Materials:**

- Your choice of yarn color
- Crochet hook size H-8

**Gauge:** Use a 5-inch gauge for this project.

Have a stylish octagon shaped center piece for your living room! Just choose the yarn color that you like and follow these easy steps.

Round 1: Make five chain stitches and slip stitch into the beginning chain to form a circle. Make three double crochets. Do fifteen double crochets on the ring. Join into the top of first double crochet with slip stitch. You should have sixteen double crochets.

Round 2: Do two double crochets in the same stitch as the chain three earlier. Make a double crochet in the following double. Make three double crochets in the following double. Make a double crochet in the following double. Repeat this until you get to the beginning of the chain.

Now, slip stitch in the top of the beginning chain. You should have thirty-two double crochets.

Round 3: Now, chain stitch three times for round three. Make three double crochets in the following double crochet, make one double crochet in the following three double crochets. Repeat until end. Make three double crochets in the following double crochet. Do one double crochet in following two. Join with slip stitch at the top of the first double crochet. Now, you should have forty-eight double crochets.

Round 4: Make three chain stitches for round four. Make a double crochet in the following double crochet. Make three double crochets in the following double crochet. Make one double crochet in the following five double. Repeat until end. Make three double crochets in the following double crochet. Make on double crochet in the following three. Join all with a slip stitch at the top beginning of the chain.

Round 5: Fasten end, cut yarn and weave using an octagon tapestry needle. Last round should make sixty-four double crochets.

## Chapter 8: Simple Amigurumi Project

## What is Amigurumi crochet?

This type of crochet is said to have originated from Japan. People would use this type of crochet when making toys that would be stuffed using this crochet. Ami means knitting or yarn that has been crocheted while amigurumi means a doll that has been stuffed. This type of crochet is therefore used when one is making these stuffed dolls through the use of heavy yarn. One can also make fan items and the large novelty cushions as well as the homewares.

# Heart Amigurumi Pattern

I've chosen a pattern that is pretty basic when it comes to amigurumi. There aren't any intricate details, whatsoever, so this project is perfect for absolute beginners. For this pattern, you can use a 2 mm crochet hook, but you may also try with a slightly bigger hook and see what looks better.

To start off, you will make a magic ring and work six single crochet (Sc) into the magic ring. Now, if you don't know how to make a magic ring, it is pretty simple.

All you need to do is to make a loop and almost as if you are making a chain pull the yarn to the front and chain one, then stitch Sc around the ring, preferably six or seven Sc and pull the yarn tail to tighten.

All you need to do is secure with a slip stitch and your first round is complete. You also need to weave in the end so that it doesn't unravel.

The reason why amigurumi start with a magic ring is that it doesn't leave a big hole in the center, unlike chaining and creating a ring out of chains. This way, you can tighten the ring as much as you would like. For the second round, you will do six increases by working two Sc into each of the Sc from the last round.

For the third round, you will work one Sc and an increase in the following. You will repeat these six times, which will result in 18 stitches at the end of the round. In the fourth round, you will crochet Sc in a Sc stitch and another in the following and then you will work an increase in the third stitch. You will repeat these six times, which will result in 24 stitches at the end of this round. In the fifth round, you will crochet seven Sc and then an increase, and repeat it two more times.

At the end of this round, you will have 27 stitches, and then for the following three rounds, Sc all the stitches. At the end of the ninth round, you will have 27 stitches. Fasten off the yarn and repeat this whole process for the second 'hump'. Once you have finished the second 'hump', do not fasten off, but join the two together. You will do this by slip stitching three of the stitches from both of the humps. This way, each of the humps will have 24 available stitches and three connected.

For the second part, you will create a wide part of the heart. You will Sc the tenth and eleventh round (48 stitches in total). Then you will begin decreasing. All the patterns will be repeated three times. For the following round, you will work 14 Sc and then one decrease.

Repeat these two more times (45 stitches in total). In the following round, you will work 13 Sc and then one decrease and again repeat these two more times (42 stitches). As you can see, a pattern arises. For each of the following rounds, you will crochet a certain number of stitches and then make a decrease and then repeat it two more times.

Each time you will decrease the number of stitches for three. It is that simple. At the end you will have six stitches. This is when you're going to insert the stuffing into your heart amigurumi and finish off the project. If you feel that it is finishing abruptly, then make another round of Sc once and decrease once, which will leave you with three stitches that can be worked together and then you can fasten off the yarn.

# Emoji Amigurumi Pattern

The following pattern is also one of the easier and simpler in terms of crocheting the basis. However, it has some finishing details that may be a bit more complicated for some people; but all in all, I think it is still one of the easiest amigurumi patterns to make.

Again, I suggest using a smaller gauge hook, but if you feel like experimenting, please do so and if you are satisfied with the outcome, keep it that way. Essentially, you will be making an amigurumi ball that by adding different finishing details will turn into emoji.

Now, let's get started! To start off, make a magic ring and work six Sc into the ring. It would be a good idea to mark the beginning of the round with a different color yarn or a stitch marker, just so that you know whether you have finished around. In the second round, you will increase in all of the stitches. In the third round, you will work one Sc and increase once, and repeat these five more times.

This way, you will increase by six stitches, 18 in total. For the fourth round, crochet two Sc and increase once, and repeat these five more times. In the fifth round, you will crochet three Sc and increase once and repeat these five more times. For the final increase, you will crochet four Sc and increase once and repeat these five more times. If you want your ball to be bigger, you can continue this way until you reach the desired size. However, we will stop increasing here and Sc all the stitches without increasing for the rounds 7-12.

Once we have done the Sc for five rounds, we will start decreasing. We will do this by reversing what we lastly did.

Now, for the 13th round, you will crochet four Sc and decrease once and repeat these five more times. In the 14th round, crochet three Sc and decrease once and repeat until the end of the round. In the 15th round, crochet two Sc and decrease once; repeat five more times. In the 16th round, crochet one Sc and decrease once.

For the final round, you will work six decreases, and finish off. But, before that, you will fill the ball with stuffing and then work the final round. Crochet all of the remained stitches together and fasten off the yarn. Of course, if you want, you can make the ball in multiple colors.

Now that you have finished the base, which is the ball, you can work on the details. For eyes, you can crochet simple round motifs. For wide-open mouth, you can crochet a semicircle, either in rows or rounds. Sew them onto the ball and embroider the black details onto the ball. You can do this either with an embroidery needle or with a crochet hook. Though if you decide to try with a crochet hook, you may find it a bit difficult and the lines will be thicker. All in all, it is a fun little project and I'm sure that you definitely need one of these. If not for your children, then it is perfect for you. I would use it as an anti-stress ball, wouldn't you?

## Chapter 9: Tips and Tricks

When you're new to something, everything might seem a tad overwhelming. Even if crocheting isn't a difficult hobby per se, this doesn't mean that it doesn't come with several challenges, especially during your first tryouts. Don't get discouraged, though, since we've all been there. What matters most is to keep going and you'll realize that you're steadily making progress.

Turn Skeins into Balls of Yarn before Starting Your Project

For one thing, you might feel impatient to get started with your very first crochet project. This might tempt you to rip the label off the skein of yarn and get started right away to see how things go. Nonetheless, even if you could crochet by using skeins of yarns, you might accomplish better results if you consider winding the skein into a ball first. As an expert, you won't tell the difference, but as a beginner, you will certainly see it.

If we were to compare balls of yarns with skeins, you should know they have several advantages. For one thing, they could help you avoid tangles. Usually, center-pull-skeins of yarn are prone to get tangled easily towards the end. On the other hand, balls of yarns don't tangle as much, which can really make the world of a difference if you want to simplify your work.

In addition to that, if you find it difficult to accomplish to right tension when crocheting, you should work from a ball of yarn as opposed to working from a ball of skein. To simplify this task, you could use ball winders – but you might also do it by hand.

Make Sure You Position the Yarn Correctly

It's always best to position the yarn correctly so that your project goes on smoothly. Basically, the ball of yarn should be positioned in such a way as to unwind easily as you crochet. Considering that you're crocheting at home from a comfortable chair, it might be a good idea to keep the ball on the floor by your feet or in your lap – depending on whichever option you prefer best.

On the other hand, if you're crocheting in a moving vehicle or in a plane, or any other place where you don't have a lot of space at your disposal, you should keep the ball inside a tote bag. This will prevent it from unwinding or rolling around.

When Needed, Change the Size of the Hook

Novice crochets have the tendency to stick to the hook they get started with. This must do, of course, with convenience and comfort. Many times, the type of hook you start to crochet with gives you a certain degree of assurance, which is why the temptation to keep using it is high. This is common not only for crochet but for other types of handwork as well, such as knitting, embroidery and the list could go on.

However, make sure you always consider the way in which your work evolves and make the necessary adjustments as you go. If you feel that your work seems too tight, you should simply switch the hook with a larger one. On the other hand, if you notice that the work appears a bit too loose, what you must do is choose a smaller crochet hook.

Essentially, the hook size written on the yarn ball is merely a suggestion and you shouldn't follow it blindly.

As a rule of thumb, before starting a project – especially a complex one – it's best to give yourself time to do some experimenting.

Nevertheless, note that changing hooks in the middle of a project is contraindicated. That's because this will make your work appear inconsistent and uneven. And you don't want that. Even if you were to use the same size hooks from different manufacturers, you would still monitor several changes when you have a closer look at your project.

At the same time, depending on the type of hook you're using, this will impact the way in which you hold it and the way in which the stitching will look in the end.

## Working on Your Tension: Why Is It So Important?

Working on your tension is important if you want to enhance your crocheting technique. In order to do this, you must keep the crochet in a way that feels comfortable – otherwise, enhancing your tension will be much more difficult. As we already pointed out, you should keep the crochet hook in the dominant hand – this depends whether you are right-handed or left-handed.

Rest assured, as a beginner to crocheting, you are bound to hold the hook either too tightly or too loosely. And while practice will most likely contribute to solving these issues, there are also some ways in which you can do that, and we'll outline them in the following paragraphs.

Pull from the center of the yarn

This could be very helpful when you feel that your tension is too loose or too tight. For example, when you pull the strand from the outside, this will make the skein bounce all over the place, which will most likely be an impediment in attaining the right level of tension. On the other hand, if you focus your attention on pulling the strand right from the center, it will glide through your fingers more easily – which will allow you to feel better about your tension.

Have a look at the way in which experts hold the hook

Although copying the technique of an expert might not be the safest solution to this tension problem, it could help. Most likely, you can have a look at numerous tutorials online and see the way in which other people use their hooks. Once you do that, you can try it yourself and see what works best for you. Remember, there are no good or wrong ways to do this. The good thing is that there are many free online resources that could get you started when you feel clueless.

Since each person works differently, if you realize that what you're looking at is not your style, you should simply look at another technique until you find someone that works in a similar way as you do.

Choose a beginner-friendly yarn

This is another useful tip if you feel that you're not making any progress. In fact, choosing a yarn that is difficult to work with might be an impediment, preventing you from making progress at a fast rate. On a different note, the tension you have when working with yarn will depend on the type of material you have chosen as well. For instance, as a beginner, your tension might be unsuitable if you're trying to work with cotton yarn, which poses some challenges to start with.

That isn't to say that all beginners will encounter difficulties when trying to work with cotton yarn, but some might. This is a subjective matter and you shouldn't feel bad or anything – it's just that when it comes to crafts, every person has his/her own rhythm of learning and progressing. This means you shouldn't put too much pressure on yourself if things are moving a bit slower than you anticipated they would.

As a rule of thumb, when you're still trying to figure out how to attain the perfect level of tension, it's best to choose a material that has a bit of stretch to it. This will make your job easier. Over time, you can diversify the types of materials you're working with, to ensure that you foster your skill and your creativity. But take your time.

In addition to that, we advise you to steer clear of novelty yarns or variegated yarns – particularly at the beginning of your crochet journey. These two types of yarns will make it especially hard to remain consistent in your stitches. Concurrently, these materials make it difficult to count the stitches, something that might be frustrating to beginners.

How to Avoid the Most Common Crochet Rookie Mistakes

Now that we've introduced some helpful tips on how to get better at crocheting, let's focus a bit on the most common mistakes you are bound to make as a rookie. Knowing these in advance can be beneficial, in the sense that you might avoid making them altogether, which will allow you to save time!

Crocheting in the front loop only

Novices to crocheting are bound to make this mistake. Therefore, we couldn't stress enough the importance of learning how to place the hook inside the stitch, as this represents the foundation of this handicraft. This mistake is likely to happen especially if the hook tends to slip from time to time and you don't realize this right away.

How do you avoid this common mistake? What you must do is simply have a closer look at the detailing of each row as you work. Basically, you should analyze each row. While this may seem tedious and time-consuming, if you practice enough, you'll get the hang of it and you won't have to do it any longer. In time, your stitches will become second nature to you, so you won't have to stress about it.

Your work seems to be getting wider and wider

This is likely to happen to anyone – beginners and advanced crocheting fans as well. Therefore, you shouldn't feel too discouraged if it seems to happen to you. This is bound to occur when you're not paying close attention to the stitches. On that note, one way to avoid this from happening is by counting your stitches – in this way, you will prevent ending up with more stitches than you had in mind when you first started working on this project.

You might be doubling up into one stitch or, without your willing, you might end up working a stitch in a turning chain. The safest and simplest way to prevent this from happening repeatedly is by counting your stitches. To that end, you might count each row as you finish, or keep an eye on the shape of your project and determine whether it is developing as you had in mind.

You might feel that this is time-consuming, but believe us; it is more time-consuming to realize that you've been working for hours in a row to realize that you've made a mistake and you have to do the entire thing all over again.

Not focusing on counting the rows while working

This mistake also has to do with maximizing your time. The same way in which it is advisable to count the stitches to the project you're doing; you should also count the rows to avoid unwanted mistakes.

When you're crocheting, you can easily get distracted, as your mind tends to wander off, especially if you're watching a TV series or anything of the kind.

Staying focused is essential if you're just starting out, so make sure you are there, in the present, when working on your project. Otherwise, you'll realize that there are five extra rows of crochet and you have lost your valuable time. You might resort to utilizing a row counter in case you end up doing the same mistake repeatedly, as it will come in handy.

# Chapter 10: Frequently Asked Questions

Here is a quick roundup of the most common questions that are asked about how to best care for your yarn or wool.

## Can you wash an entire skein?

In some cases, you may need to wash the skeins or yarn balls before use (spillages etc.) and although this can be difficult it is possible. The trickiest part about this is to ensure that the yarn doesn't unravel which you can do by putting it in a pair of tights or washing bag beforehand. However, make sure to follow the same washing guidelines and check to see that all detergent has been rinsed out (you may need to hand rinse them to make sure as this could cause irritation if there is residue)

## How often should you wash yarn or wool?

This depends on the amount of wear and the purpose of the project. For example, a crochet bag may only need to be sponged down once in a while whereas clothes would need to be washed more frequently. Clothes such as socks would definitely need to be washed after each use to avoid any fungal or bacterial infections while a jumper may be worn a few times before needing to be washed. It entirely depends.

## Can you dye your own yarn?

The answer to this is yes and the easiest types of yarn to dye are those that are animal fibers, for example alpaca, wool or mohair. Make sure to protect your skin and clothes when dying your own yarn as it easily transfers and can cause a large mess. For synthetic yarn you will need to buy specific dye to use for the fiber.

## How do you find yarn care instructions for other yarn?

Usually, yarn will come with a wraparound label that has specific washing instructions on the outside or overleaf of the label. Some special types of yarn will come with packet instructions and others may not come with anything at all. The more specialized the yarn is, the more likely you are to get instructions. Generally speaking, worsted weight yarn which is most commonly used is also more durable which means you are less likely to get specific instructions.

## Can you get rid of old stains and smells?

Yes, however not always and a lot of dried on stains or lingering smells are hard to get rid of. The longer the stain or smell has been present on the fiber, the harder it is to get rid of.

## Can you tumble dry?

It is best not to tumble dry yarn or wool as it is very sensitive to temperature and it can make it rough or coarse on the skin (as well as risk of shrinking) if it is exposed to higher temperatures. If you choose to use the tumble dryer it is best to do so on a cool or very low heat setting for short amounts at a time to check it is not having adverse effects on the fibers.

## How long can you keep yarn or wool for?

Wool or yarn can be kept for a very long time over a range of years if it is stored properly in the right conditions and maintained. Wool that has been kept for over 10 years may not be viable for crocheting or knitting because it has started to degrade but this depends on the type. Organic fibers that haven't been treated may not last as long as store-bought that have been chemically treated.

# How do you store yarn?

Store In skeins or balls in a dry place and make sure to clean out and check frequently to avoid your stash coming into contact with a lot of dust, moths or pests that might contaminate the supply. In addition, avoid getting your stash wet and ensure that you frequently air it out to avoid there being a musty smell embedded in the yarn.

## How to Read Crochet Patterns?

To my opinion, reading a pattern of crochet is important for learning simple crochet. You are very limited when it comes to finished projects unless you can read crochet patterns!

**If you can't read a pattern for a crochet, I think you are very tight. What are you doing, keep going until you think it is right and start like that?**

You have the world at your fingertips if you can read a crochet pattern. You're not afraid to try new stuff in my opinion!

However, I am fascinated by the number of people who cannot understand crochet patterns. It seems like a real shame that they don't know how to get better and feel better about their efforts!

**If you cannot read a pattern of crochet, how do you make home-made dishcloths or crochets? Remember; in the picture they look fast, but can you double that?**

When I started to crochet (it seems to have been a lifetime), these patterns with such unusual abbreviations were a challenge for me. At this point, I decided to learn how to read the patterns regardless.

I have done a lot of work and answered a variety of questions and have eventually obtained results. The odd thing was that even I wasn't even crocheting wool alone.

To be able to read crochet patterns would seem to encourage you to go higher—that's how I switched to cotton and made doilies in a very short time learning how to read patterns from crochet.

What scares me is that people who can't read crochet patterns don't seem to be careful to clarify and/or illustrate any of the crochet stitches on a one-on - one basis. This disturbs me.

I was told that it demonstrated a lack of maturity in someone who did crochet home in that way not to be able to read crochet patterns. It did not have any ambition!

Now I'm not in agreement, but I've got one I can tell—"Don't learn something at the half, learn the whole thing, or waste my time!" I could crochet a doily while my oldest daughter was in the hospital at the age of five (5) months, by reading crochet instructions.

Here is another thing to consider:

How do you increase your own crocheting skills to include extra stitches if you can't read crochet instructions or patterns? I mean the triple stitch, the half double stitch and so on—it could be overwhelming!

And if you're a home crocheter, learn how to read the patterns that I call never-ending, extend your scope beyond your standards.

# Conclusion

Thank you for making it to the end. Finishing what you have woven is an achievement. The following step is to work your way through the techniques, so you can improve your skills in crocheting.

But before you get started on your projects, remember that it is important not to cut the strand flush with the knot after sewing. Because of repetitive use and washing, the cut knot would end up falling apart and could ruin what you have woven. For this, it is necessary that you leave enough thread to hide it and finish off the project well.

This also occurs with all strands derived from the junctions of clews and others. This type of thread trim will serve you both if you have knitted with the reverse of a jersey stitch. That said you also have to know that there is a multitude of different methods to join strands of clews. Here is a basic way of joining two clews:

1. Join on the edge of the work.

2. With the strand of the new skein, make a simple knot by wrapping the strand of the used skein. When you are knitting, there are times when you finish a ball, and you have to join with the beginning of another ball to continue knitting. The first thing you have to know is that never are

two balls joined in the middle of knitted work. It is necessary to unite in the borders, that is to say, at the beginning or at the end of a turn (although it seems to you that you are wasting wool).

3.  Adjust that knot bringing it as close as possible to the needle (the new skein is now attached)

4.  Make a knot between the strand of the skein used and the strand of the new skein (now the strand used is attached).

5.  Start knitting with the new strand.

We hope you have at least learned the basics of crocheting. With some practice, hard work and dedication, you will master crocheting. There is no talent required for crocheting; it is just the passion and interest that will make you the expert in crocheting. There are even young children and adults who are now crocheting. It is all about practice. Some mistakes and failures will come your way while crocheting. But you should not get discouraged by it. All you need is continuously practicing, and with time you will master the art.

Crochet beginners and experts alike enjoy creating projects from patterns. Although it is possible to use the beginner stitches and make a blanket without a pattern, a pattern will provide more detail. Some patterns use small crochet appliques or alternating patterns and the project patterns show how to do it.

Many crocheters learn to make their own patterns and graphs from the abbreviations and symbols they have learned. Once you master all of the stitches you will be able to make your own patterns so others can make project you have designed.

Using patterns may seem difficult and overwhelming at first but once you are used to seeing the abbreviations and symbols your skills will improve. Stick to patterns and graphs for beginners, these use beginner stitches, so you can learn at your own pace.

Learning the skill to read and follow graphs and patterns will allow you to create more than just a scarf or simple throw. You will be able to complete heirloom quality projects, winter clothing such as sweaters, mittens, gloves, hats and scarfs, dresses, home décor such as doilies or place mats and runners, and even toys for the kids.

Use your new-found ability to make gifts for loved ones and friends alike. Everyone enjoys receiving a handmade item that is useful and beautiful. No matter what you decide to make, the time and effort you put into the creation will show in the finished product.

So, as you can see from this guide, crocheting is a skill that is easy to pick up, and fun to master. Once you have gotten to grips with each stitch and technique, working out patterns will quickly become natural and then you can create whatever you want, including your very own patterns.

Crocheting is a brilliant way to create unique, homemade gifts, with a personal touch, or even cute little additions to spice up your own home or wardrobe. There isn't a better feeling than creating something yourself, and seeing others admire it!

There are many amazing resources online for crocheter – in fact, there is quite a huge community of web pages and forums where users can share their tips and tricks. This is a great way to discover ore about your new skill, whilst meeting new people from all over the world and making friends. Once you have the ability to crochet, you won't look back!

Before you start crocheting, you have to take into account a series of tips that will make your life as a weaver much easier than you think. As you go above the needles and find a position that is comfortable for you to wear the strand when knitting, you will gradually relax, let go of the knitting, and find your own "tension of weaver."

When you start crocheting, it is often so overwhelming that the wool escapes between your fingers, the needles are drained, and the stitches are released while crocheting. This insecurity that causes us to face something new makes us weave the point very tightly. It's totally normal for this to happen, and you don't have to get overwhelmed or give it a lot of importance. You're not going to weave that tight always.

But until that happens, it is advisable to start crocheting with the right needles. So, what are the right needles when you start? The first thing you should know is that there are no good needles or bad needles in themselves. In principle, each type of needle is designed for a type of fiber and a type of weaver.

But when you start for the first time, you have to keep in mind that the needles offer some resistance and make them "break" the stitches on them a bit. This will make it harder for you to slip the stitches of the needle and to escape it, giving you better control above what you are doing. And for this, the needles that offer more resistance are bamboo.

Therefore, when you start crocheting, it is good that you start with this type of needles, so you can knit more comfortably. But as you learn, it is ideal to try different types of needles.

The first time you are going to try, and since you have never done it until now, your first instinct is a color that you can combine well with your clothes. I don't know why this happens, but the first thing that comes to mind is to choose dark wool (black, brown, navy blue, etc.), thinking that we can give more use to what we are going to weave because we can combine it better with our closet bottom.

I hope this was able to give you the inspiration you need to start crocheting, and that you take the skills you have learned here and show them off to the world. As with any new craft, practice makes perfect, and the more you work at this, the better you are going to become.

Have fun and please…leave me an honest review!

# Knitting for beginners

The A-Z guide to knitting patterns and stitches with pictures and illustrations. How to enjoy yourself while at home even if you are a beginner

# Introduction

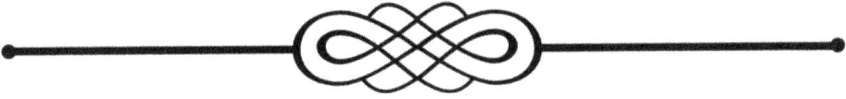

Knitting is the process which produces cloth from thread. It's used to create garments, toys, home wares and all sorts of exciting things! It's a skill that can be enjoyed by anyone – and it's growing in popularity every single day with celebrities such as Sarah Jessica Parker and Cameron Diaz happily declaring their love for the hobby. But, it's actually so much more than that. Knitting can be beneficial to your health! It has been proven to lower blood pressure, relax the enthusiast and even burn calories (approximately 55 for half an hour of knitting).

In fact, knitting has become so popular that there are now many competitions and challenges associated with it. The most well-known of these being:

The World's Fastest Knitter – currently held by Miriam Toggles of the Netherlands who can hand knit 118 stitches in one minute.

Speed Knitting – currently held by Linda Benne of America who can knit 253 stitches in 3 minutes.

The World Knitting Record – currently held by Australia at 4 hours and 50 minutes.

Of course, these aren't things that we are aiming for just yet! They are just interesting facts which demonstrate how widespread knitting has become. Although these days it is considered a hobby more popular with females, knitting started out as a male only occupation, proving that anyone can reap the benefits from it!

There are many suggestions of when knitting began, but the truth of it is no one really knows since numerous antique textile fragments believe to be knitting have actually transformed out to be an ancient form of needle craft, often thought of single needle knitting – nalbinding. However, when the knitting machine was invented, hand knitting became less of an essential necessity, and more of a hobby, which is where we are at today.

'Knitting for Beginners' is an extensive guide to the basics of knitting – giving you step-by-step instructions helping you to master all of the stitches and techniques that you'll need to get started with this brand-new skill. Once you have gotten to grips with some of these, a few patterns have been included which will get you putting everything together in fun and interesting ways. Once you have completed these – anything else will become much easier in comparison.

In fact, this is the most comprehensive knitting guide for beginners available on the market, and once you have worked through everything within its pages, you'll never look back!

Knitting was mainly done on silk, wool, and other fibers that decompose Quickly, even in the most controlled, most excellent conditions. Knitting needles are just an ordinary pair of honed sticks and could have been anything, a pair of hair picks, skewers, maybe spindles, or any of the other million uses you could think of sharpened sticks; so it's really difficult to identify them as actual knitting needles beyond any reasonable doubt.

Knitted items in the past were all done by hand and yarn, a valuable item, was not disposed until it has completely worn out to the point of disintegrating. Knitted sweaters that do not fit anymore can easily be unraveled and re-knitted over and over again. Not many people had the brilliant idea to save their everyday items for their children. Leaving heirlooms was not a major consideration.

Because of these factors, no one really knows the exact origins of knitting. It's all a huge mystery; and with solid evidences missing, there are not that many valuable knitted items left for us to discover. All experts, and the rest of us, can do is make intelligent guesses derived from fragments and scraps found in museums around the world.

Linguistically speaking, knitting is a fairly fresh invention. The Oxford Unabridged English Dictionary says that the term 'to knit' which means 'to make loops with two long and straight needles' was only added to the English language in the 14th century. The term 'to knit' did not appear in any European language before the Renaissance.

While it's true that knitting has not been around for very long, and that its past is quite bunched up in knots, pun intended; one thing remains. That thing which had made knitting an instant hit when it was invented and makes it popular today is its sheer simplicity. With two sticks and a ball of yarn, you can literally make anything; sweaters, gloves, socks, scarves, bonnets and hats, bags, and so much more. Knitwear is as just as popular as ever before. Even science has jumped on the bandwagon. Engineers are now using knitting techniques for metallic shields for hoses and doctors are starting to knit nylon arteries used to transplant organs. One thing is for sure; Knitting may not have a solid past but it has a bright future ahead of it.

The Health Benefits of Knitting

Knitting has existed for many centuries; first and foremost, as a way to survive. In its purest and earliest form, knitting sprouted from the basic human need to protect the body against heat, cold, and other elements.

Many centuries, with the many ready to wear and cheaper, not to mention easier options; humans do not depend on making their clothes by hand. With a short trip to the mall and a flick of small plastic card, you can get any type of handmade or machine made clothing you want.

Knitting, today, is no longer a necessity; however, over the years, it has gathered a huge following who take up the craft as a hobby. Why shouldn't they? Besides the obvious advantage of making your own useful and unique articles and garments, knitters also enjoy physical and psychological health benefits from knitting.

- Knitting helps you clear your mind by engaging your brain in a creative activity and helping your forget the stresses and anxieties you experience every day.

- The rhythmic motion you follow when knitting has been expertly proven to change the brain's movement; releasing good hormones such as serotonin and dopamine which makes you feel happy and relaxed.

- These rhythmic repetitive movements also helps distract knitters from mulling over the past and pondering about the future. Knitting helps keep you in the moment. The relaxation response is not only good for your psychological well-being; it is also good for your physical health as it is known to control blood pressure, heart rate and prevent stress related sickness.

- Moving your eyes from side to side is also helpful. Therapists using Eye Movement Desensitization and Reprocessing (EMDR) have proven that moving your eyes from side to side or rolling your eyes is a potent yoga exercise and has worked wonders with trauma patients.

- The learning process involved in knitting helps you feel good about yourself and helps improve your self-esteem. Studies also show that as you learn and master more complicated stitches, you gain the confidence to try out new things in other aspects of your life.

- Through knitting, you will be accustomed to following and identifying patterns, learning new movements, using both your hands, and yes, even learning math. It helps improve fine motor skills and keeps the mind active. Knitting develops dexterity, concentration and basic arithmetic.

- Knitting, as well as other crafts, engages both body and mind. This causes optimistic feelings about life in general. As surveys have proven, knitters are inclined to be more sociable, friendly, positive, and outgoing.

Besides having a one of a kind knitted article that you invested blood, sweat and tears on, the health benefits of knitting are also outstanding. Knitting in the ancient times was a way for people to survive. Knitting now is a way for people to stay alive, happy, and healthy. Many centuries have come and gone but one thing remains; we are still knitting for our lives. Start your wonderful knitting journey today.

# Chapter 1: Knitting Supplies: Tools and Materials

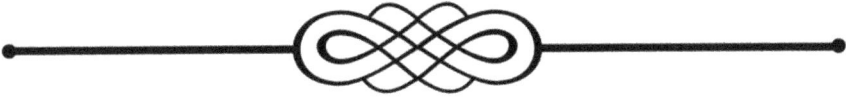

## Needles

A knitting needle, also referred to as knitting pin, is a tool with an elongated shaft and taper at the end, used for making knitted fabrics. A typical knitting needle has two functions; the pointed ends are used to create new stitches, while the long shaft clutches running stitches to avoid unscrambling. To describe the size of a knitting needle, the first parameter to consider is its diameter, while the second is its length. The diameter of the needle determines the size of a new stitch, while the length determines the number of stitches that the needle can hold at a time. More often than not, knitters use needles with the same diameter for a single project. However, some projects require uneven knitting; for such projects, needles of different sizes are used.

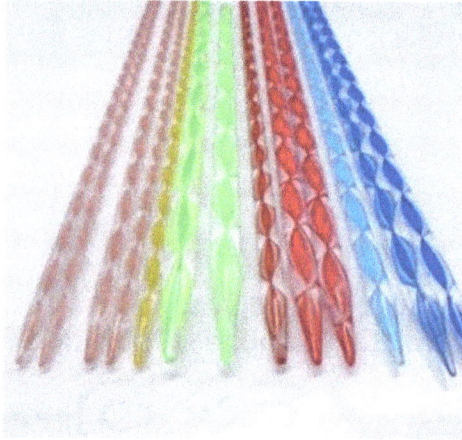

## Types of Knitting Needles

There are different types, size and materials of needles used in knitting. These different types of needles have unique properties and are ideal for diverse yarn types and projects. Let's consider the common types of knitting needles.

### Single-pointed or Straight Knitting Needles

This is the most typical type of needle, and most people picture straight needles when they think about knitting needles. More often than not, single-pointed needles come in sets of two. One end of a straight needle is pointed, while the other end is not. Due to its ease of use, straight needles are ideal for beginner knitters. The length of a characteristic straight needle is between 9 to 14 inches; however, there are longer and shorter needles.

The most common materials used for producing straight needles are wood, bamboo, aluminum, steel, and plastic. Knitting needles made from each of these materials have their unique characteristics, as well as their pros and cons. If your stitches slide off your needles too quickly, you need to try another set of needles made from a different material.

Straight needles are most suitable for small projects like scarves, squares, among others, that only require flat knitting.

**Double-Pointed Knitting Needles**

This type of knitting needle usually come in sets of four, five or six, and it is mostly used for knitting small circular or semi-circular projects. A typical double-pointed knitting needle is between 5 to 8 inches long. While the shorter needles are ideal for smaller projects like gloves, socks, among others, the longer needles are suitable for tube-shaped projects like sweater sleeves, hats, among others. It takes more time to learn to work with double-pointed knitting needles than straight needles; however, learning how to use double-pointed needles is profitable because they are a suitable option for knitting small projects in the round.

## A particular type of double-pointed knitting needle is the cable needle.

It is usually short and mostly used to hold some stitches for a period when the knitter wants to form a cable pattern. Cable needles may be U-shaped or have a U-shaped curve. This bend helps to disallow falling off of stitches while the cable pattern is being made with the primary needle.

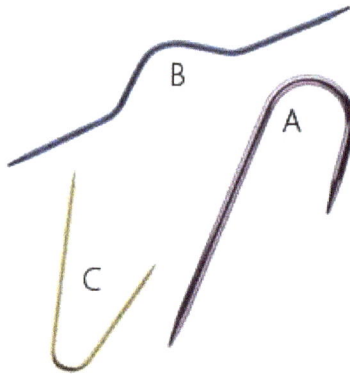

### Circular Knitting Needles

These knitting needles typically have two sharp, straight points linked by a flexible cable. They can be used for both flat and circular knitting. Circular knitting needles come in different lengths, sizes and are made with diverse materials like aluminum, plastic, nickel-plated brass, and steel. The two-pointed ends of a circular knitting needle allow for easy knitting and can be about 4 to 5 inches long. The length of a typical circular knitting needle is between 16 and 48 inches. Circular knitting needles are primarily used for round knitting of projects like hats, seaters socks, among others. However, they can also be used for flat projects like shawls, blankets, among others, which are usually very difficult with straight needles.

**Interchangeable Knitting Needles**

These needles allow for flexibility of using circular needles with different sizes, and in different ways. Interchangeable needles have a flexible cord and a firm tip and are designed such that it is easy to alter the cord lengths and needle sizes. They can also be used as straight needles when needles and connected to the cords and caps attached to the ends. Interchangeable knitting needles come as individual pieces or in sets.

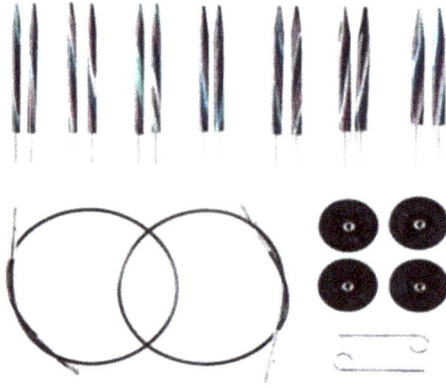

**Other tools**

### Stitch Markers

These are materials (small rings, metal, or plastic) that can be placed between stitches to delineate a crucial part in your chosen knitting pattern. The two common types of stitch markers are ring and locking. Ring stitch markers are solid circles while locking stitch markers open and close with a bolt. Stitch markers can be used to mark the beginning of a round, the start and finish of a color chart repeat, points where patterns repeat in a lace, points where knitting tension is increased or decreased, points where cable and other special stitches begin and end, among others.

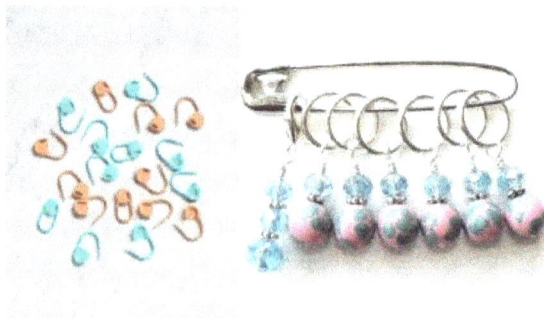

**Knitting Bag**

This is used mainly for keeping or storing knitting tools and accessories. You must keep your tools to prevent damage to them. Knitting needles and yarns, for example, need safe storage, and the knitting bag can be an excellent material for that. You can make a knitting bag yourself to suit your need or purchase an already made knitting bag.

**Point Protectors**

They are little rubber caps that are used to prevent stitches from falling of knitting needles after knitting. Point protectors are made in diverse sizes and styles.

**Row Counter**

Row counter is a knitting tool that helps to keep track of the number of rows you've knitted. It is easy to forget if you are counting the number of rows yourself; however, with a row counter, you can allow your brain to think about other things. The only thing is you have to remember to push it up after knitting each row.

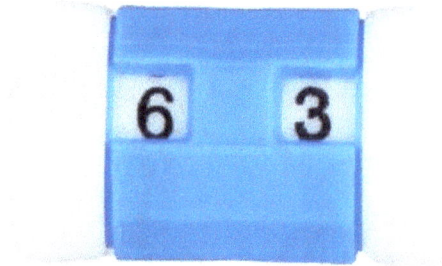

**Tape Measure**

When knitting, there's always one thing or the other to measure. As such, it is crucial to have a measuring tape at your disposal before you begin any knitting project.

Knitting needles come in three main types: straight needles (come in various lengths and have a tip at one end and a knob on the other), circular needles (having two needles connected by a cord of nylon, come in a variety of lengths) and double-pointed needles (with tips at both ends, sold in groups of four or five).

## Straight Needles

Most knitters begin with straight needles. For beginners who start with small projects, such as scarves, these needles are the best complement. The size to be used is chosen according to the thickness of the yarn and the type of stitch with which it will be knitted. Many times, the number of recommended needles is indicated on yarn labels. They are used to make woven, working with a row of points moving a needle to the other, turning the work to the end row (the needle containing the points again in the left hand is placed) and beginning again.

## Circular Needles

Circular needles consist of a pair of single pointed needles joined by a nylon cord. When knitting with circular needles, you get a seamless piece, a tubular fabric, ideal for when you create a hat or the body of a sweater. Circular needles come in different lengths: 30, 40, 50, 60, 80,

100, 120 and 150 cm. They can also be used for flat fabrics such as with straight needles. They are very useful for projects with lots of points such as blankets, ponchos and shawls. Many weavers who venture with the use of the circular are then their favorite needles.

## Knitting with Circular Needles

Circular knitting needles are another sensation that has taken the yarn-crafting world by storm and with good reason. They are fun to use and easy to carry. They are usually made using the same materials used to make straight knitting needles, i.e., resin, plastic, metal, and bamboo. Two of the hard-knitting tips are connected using a flexible cord, which holds the stitches. Using the right needle length suited to your project is crucial because the number of stitches needs to fit on the needle comfortably. Knitting in the round means that you will be knitting on the front of the fabric or the right side the whole time. Circular stitching is mostly done with a stockinette stitch, meaning that all you will need to do is knit each row. To create a garter stitch with circular needles, you will have to knit one row and purl the other.

Circular needles can also be used to knit flat, which can be beneficial when you are working on a huge project such as a throw, wrap, or afghan. Circular needles hold the stitches somewhat better, and they make things easier for you as the needles hold most of the knitting project's weight. Keep in mind that knitting flat using circular needles is not the same as knitting using straight needles. You will not join in the round, but instead, you will simply cast on and knit from the left needle to the right as you typically would with straight needles. Once you get to the end of one row, alternate hands as normal.

You can learn how to knit with a crochet hook using a tool known as a Knook. It is a tool designed to make knitted fabrics but looks a lot like a conventional crochet hook. One can also crochet any fabric that seems to be knitted using the Tunisian knit stitch. The right side of the Tunisian Knit stitch is similar to knitting and tends to curl up just as the stocking/stockinette stitch does. The Tunisian knit stitch is usually done using a long crochet hook that resembles a Tunisian hook or afghan hook. The hook looks like a knitting needle but with a hook at one end.

## Double Point Needles

The double-pointed needles are used in groups of four or five. They serve to work in the round as with circular needles, but these have a tip at each end. To use double-pointed needles, the stitches are distributed evenly over three needles (sometimes over four) and the remaining needle is used to work the stitches. They are practical for knitting small projects such as socks, caps or gloves. Double-pointed needles are purchased in groups of 4 or 5 needles and in lengths of 10 to 25 cm.

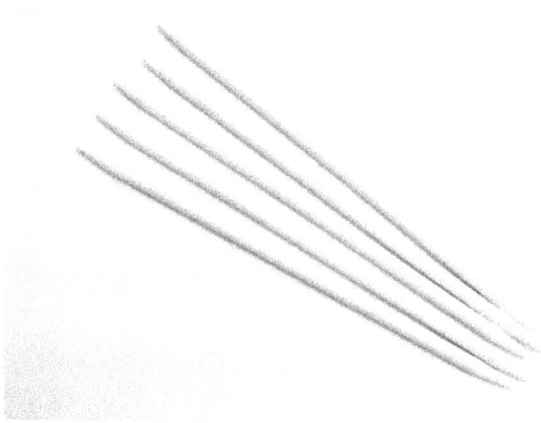

## Auxiliary Needle

It is a small needle with tips at both ends; usually about 10cm long and some have a twist or crank in the center to help the stitches not fall off the needle. They are used to temporarily suspend stitches that have been removed from the working needle and will be knitted. The points suspended on the auxiliary needle can be placed on the front or the back of the work (the pattern always indicates to which side the points are suspended).

## Auxiliary Hook

It is used to reserve numerous points that you need to work in the other time (like a vest), they usually look like large hook pins with blunt tips. You can use a pin to suspend a small number of stitches.

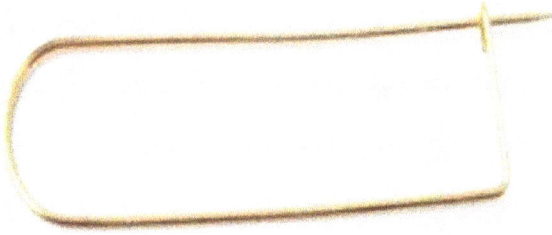

## Wool Sewing Needle

It is a needle with a very large buttonhole and the rounded tip used to sew between stitches.

## Crochet Needle

Crochet needles, known as crochet hooks, are between 12 and 17 cm long, with a hook at one end, which is used to hook the thread and pull it through the stitches. The crochet is held by the handle that usually has a flat part that serves as a grip. Some designs have on the opposite end of the hook some ornaments or other hook, but these are decorative and do not fulfill any function. In knitwear, a crochet needle is useful for rescuing dots.

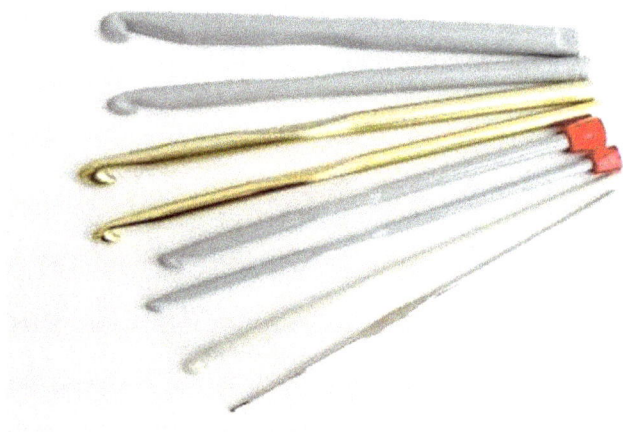

## Chapter 2: Types of Yarn

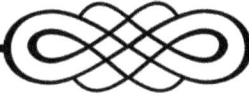

### Single or One-Ply Yarns

Single yarns contain a single strand of fiber, which is held together by twisting. Single yarns could also include grouped filaments, irrespective of the twist. Single yarns that contain several short fibers are usually held either by the S-twist or Z-twist. Singe yarns are essential in knitting because they are most suitable for an enormous variety of fabrics.

# A single yarn.

### Ply Yarns

Ply or folded yarns are made by twisting combined preferably two single yarns. There are diverse types of ply yarns. They include double

-ply yarn, which contains two strands of single yarns; and three-ply yarns, which comprises three strands of single yarns, among others. Ply yarns are most suitable for making heavy industrial fabrics and delicate-looking sheer fabrics.

## Cord Yarns

Cord yarns are made when ply yarns are twisted together. In this case, the twist of the cord yarn is usually in the opposite direction to the twist of the ply yarns. The common types of cord yarns are cable cords and hawser cord. Cord yarns are mostly used as ropes and twines. Also, they can be used to produce heavy industrial fabrics as well as sheer dress fabrics.

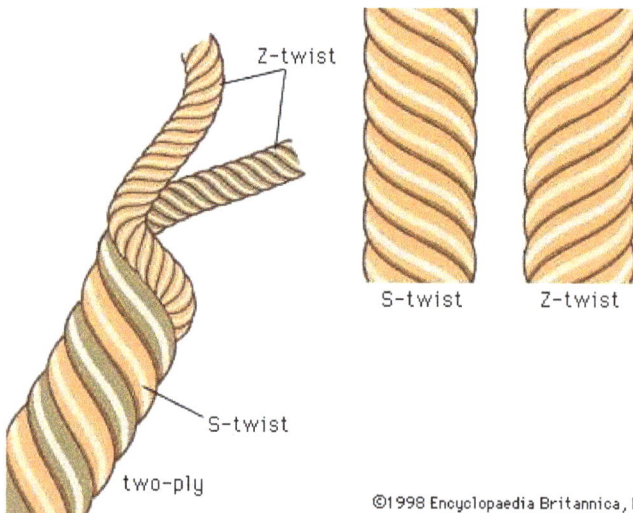

©1998 Encyclopaedia Britannica, Inc.

## Novelty Yarns

Novelty yarns are made of synthetic yarn blends. They are usually introduced during production to achieve particular effects such as crimping and texturizing. The common types of novelty yarns are Bouclé, Chenille, Thick-thin, Faux fur, Railroad ribbon, among others.

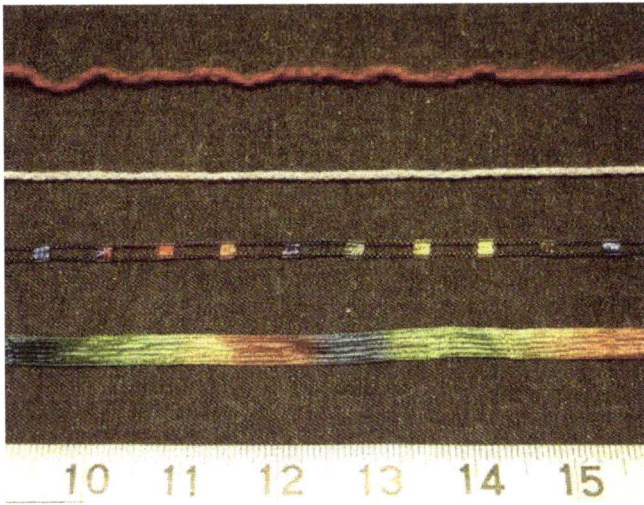

**Types of Yarn Fibers**

Yarns, used for knitting, are made from fibers from different sources, which could be animal-based, plant-based, or synthetic. Yarns from different fibers have different characteristics and qualities. However, manufacturers often blend different types of yarn fiber to create a desired effect or remove an undesirable condition. Let's look at the different types of yarn fibers in more detail.

**Animal-Based Yarn Fibers**

Animal-based yarn fiber, otherwise referred to as wool, is obtained from sheep, goats, and some other animals. Many knitters prefer using wool to other types of yarn fibers for several projects. Its durability, and insulative capacity makes it the best for making winter garments. Wool comes in different characteristics depending on the animal that produces the wool. However, some people are allergic to some kings of wool. Wools can be categorized into four based on their sizes. They are wool type fine, wool type medium, wool type long, and wool type double coated. Wool is said to be pure or virgin when it is made directly from animal fleece.

**Wool is fleeced from different animals; therefore, there are several types. Some of the popular ones are tackled as follows.**

### Merino wool

This type of wool is fleeced from a breed of sheep called the Merino Sheep. It is commonly used in knitting big, chunky items. The prominent feature of the Merino wool is that it is very soft and does not induce allergic reactions. Fabrics made with Merino wool don't lose shape when blocked. However, Merino can create pilling, also called little fuzzballs, and they can be a bit annoying. When you are thinking of doing extreme knitting, think of using Merino wool.

**Cashmere**

This type of wool is derived from the shoulders and backs of Kashmir goats. In the past, Cashmere was only available to royalty. However, in recent times, more knitters have come to appreciate this yarn fiber. Cashmere is very expensive because Kashmir goats shed their undercoat only once in a year. Unlike sheep that is shorn, Kashmir goats' undercoat is combed and collected in a very labor-intensive process. To make a sweater with Cashmere, you need fibers collected from about four goats. Cashmere is suitable for knitting clothing, because it is soft and does not itch.

**Alpaca Fleece**

This wool is derived from the South American Alpaca. It is very soft and silky; however, the fabrics made from it don't hold their shape like other types of wools. There are diverse kinds of Alpaca Fleece, but Huacaya and Suri are the commonest ones. Alpaca fleece usually comes in blue and lime green colors, and it is ideal for knitting sweaters. Alpaca Fleece is often classier and more expensive than the regular types of wool. The yarn can be light or weighty, depending on how it is spun. It is also water and fire-resistant.

**Llama Fleece**

is derived from the Llama, and it is similar in characteristics to the Alpaca Fleece. A Llama produces two layers of fleece. The inner coat is mostly used for making clothing, while the outer skin is usually used for making ropes and rugs.

### Benefits of Knitting with Wool Yarn

Some of the advantages of using wool yarn over other fiber sources are tackled below.

Resistant to Wrinkling: Due to the coil-like structure of wool, it is incredibly elastic. If you stretch a sweater made of wool, it jolts back to its original shape as soon as you release it. When wet and dry, wool can be stretched up to 50% and 30% respectively, and yet bounce back to its initial shape. Also, wool yarn is the best for fitted projects and products that may require a little stretch like indoor footwear, gloves, among others.

Durability: Wool's flexibility makes it less likely to tear, and thus, more durable than other fibers. In fact, wool is 7 and 10 times stronger than Cotton and silk respectively. The outer skin of the wool also serves as protection against abrasion.

Ease of use: For beginner knitters, wool yarn is ideal for projects. Its flexibility makes it easier to ensure consistency in the knitting tension, which is very crucial to having an excellent end product.

Water and fire resistant: Due to the structure of wool, which consists of minuscule overlapping scales, and the lanolin from the animal that produced the wool, it can almost be waterproof. Also, moisture is present within each fiber of wool, thereby making it less susceptible to fire.

Sustainability and Renewability: Wool has been shorn from sheep and other animals since time immemorial, and it has never finished, because the animals keep producing them year in, year out. Also, the yarn and products made from wool are biodegradable. Thus, they don't cause pollution to the environment, unlike some other fibers.

### Disadvantages of Knitting with Wool Yarn

The major drawback of knitting with wool yarn is that several people react negatively to wool. Also, some people are allergic to lanolin, which is present in sheep that produce wool. However, if you are making a product for people that have these allergies, you can consider using other types of wool like the merino wool yarn.

### Plant-based Yarn Fibers

Generally, products made from plant-based yarn fibers do not give insulation as much as products from animal-based yarn fibers. However, products from plant-based yarn fibers can absorb moisture and are usually more breathable. Furthermore, products from plant-based yarn fibers have hypoallergenic properties. Let's discuss some of the common plants that produce yarn for knitting.

## Cotton fiber

This is a light and absorbent yarn fiber derived from the cotton plant, which is mostly grown in warm climates. The biggest producers of Cotton are USA, India, and China. Standard colors of cotton yarn are shades of pink, green, and yellow. When compared with wool, Cotton does not offer sufficient elasticity. To offset this undesirable quality, cotton is often blended with nylon. When placed in water, Cotton can absorb up to 27 times its weight, and is most suitable for knitting tops and tanks to be used in summer. There are three significant types of cotton fiber available for knitting purposes – the Egyptian fiber, which is the smoothest, softest, and longest; the American fiber, which has several color varieties, and is the most popular; and the Pima, which results from crossing the American and Egyptian cotton fibers.

## Bamboo fiber

This is a renewable, biodegradable resource, also called "green" yarn. It is suitable for making clothing for warm weather because of its breathability and coolness. It is lightweight, soft, and has non-allergenic properties. Bamboo fiber yarn has antibacterial properties, and a beautiful drape; it is, therefore, ideal for garments that require drape. When spun into yarn, Bamboo fiber is softer than silk.

**Linen fiber**

This is an excellent material for making clothing that could be used in summer. Of all plant-based yarn fibers, it is the most durable against hotness. Despite the great attributes of Linen fiber, its major setback is that it wrinkles easily.

**Silk fiber**

This is a plant-based yarn fiber that is mostly used for making summer clothing. It is arguably the most versatile fiber, that offers warm insulation for winter and cool breathability during hot weather. It is most suitable for knitting blankets and children's garments. Spun silk yarn and Reeled silk yarn are the significant types of silk yarn available.

**seidentraum.biz**

## Synthetic Yarn Fibers

These are yarns made from chemicals. One general characteristic of yarn fibers under this category is that knitters can maintain them without much stress. Let's get into the details of the different types of synthetic yarn fibers.

### Acrylic yarn

is less expensive than wool, and this makes it very suitable for use by beginner knitters. Acrylic yarn is great for pets' accessories and baby clothing. It is color-fast, washes easily, and is ideal for multi-color yarn braids. However, clothing made from acrylic yarns reacts negatively to oils, moths, sunlight, and chemicals.

**Metallic yarn**

is a synthetic fiber that is made up of metal-coated plastic, plastic-coated metal, or a core entirely shielded by metal. Metallic yarn is suitable for adding glitz to your knitted fabrics.

## Chapter 3: Glossary Terms

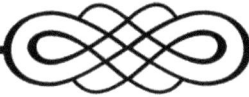

# Knit abbreviations

| ABBREVIATION | DESCRIPTION |
| --- | --- |
| * | Repeat starting point (i.e., repeat from *) |
| ** | Repeat all instructions between asterisks |
| ( ) | Alternate measurements and/or instructions |
| [ ] | Instructions that are to be worked as a group a specified number of times |
| ALT | alternate(ing) |
| APPROX. | approximately |
| BEG | beginning |
| C4B | Slip 2 stitches onto cable needle and leave at back of work. K2, then K2 from cable needle |

| ABBREVIATION | DESCRIPTION |
| --- | --- |
| C4F | Slip 2 stitches onto cable needle and leave at front of work. K2, then K2 from cable needle |
| CL | K2tog. Keep stitches on left-hand needle. P2tog into the same stiches. Slip off left-hand needle |
| CM | centimeter(s) |
| CO | cast on |
| CONT | continue(ity) |
| DEC | decrease(ing) |
| DTR | double treble |
| G | gram(s) |
| INC | increase 1 stitch by knitting into front and back of succeeding stitch |
| K | Knit |
| K1BELOW | knit into succeeding stitch 1 row below |
| K1TBL | Knit succeeding stitch through back of loop |
| K2TOG | Knit 2 stitches together |
| K2TOGTBL | Knit 2 stitches together through back loops |
| K3(4, N) TOG | Knit succeeding 3(4, n) stitches together |
| KFB | increase 1 stitch by knitting into front and back of succeeding stitch |

| ABBREVIATION | DESCRIPTION |
|---|---|
| M1 | Make 1 stitch by picking up horizontal loop lying before succeeding stitch and knitting into back of loop. |
| M1P | Make 1 stitch by picking up horizontal loop lying before succeeding stitch and purling into back of loop. |
| MB | Make bobble: [(K1. yfwd) 3 times. K1] all in succeeding st. Turn. P7. Turn. Sl1. K1. psso. K3. K2tog. Turn. P2tog. P1. P2togtbl. Turn. Sl1. K2tog. psso - bobble made |
| MM | millimeter(s) |
| OZ | ounce(s) |
| P | purl |
| P2TOG | purl two stitches together |
| P3(4, N) TOG | purl succeeding 3(4, n) stitches together |
| P2TOGTBL | purl 2 stitches together through back loops |
| PAT | pattern |
| PSSO | pass slipped stitch over |
| REM | remain(ing) |
| REP | repeat |
| RND(S) | round(s) |
| RS | right side |
| SL ST | Slip stitch |

| ABBREVIATION | DESCRIPTION |
| --- | --- |
| SL1 | Slip succeeding stitch knitwise |
| SL1K | Slip succeeding stitch knitwise |
| SL1P | Slip succeeding stitch purlwise |
| SSK | Slip succeeding 2 stitches knitwise one at a time. Pass them back onto left-hand needle, then knit through back loops together |
| ST | stockinette stitch |
| ST(S) | stitch(es) |
| TOG | together |
| WS | wrong side |
| YB | bring yarn into back of work |
| YF | bring yarn into front of work |
| YFWD | yarn forward (makes 1 extra stitch) |
| YO | yarn over the needle (makes 1 extra stitch) |
| YON | yarn over needle (same as yo - makes 1 extra stitch) |
| YRN | yarn round needle (makes 1 extra stitch) |

**Knit glossary**

Attached I Cord: A thick, cord-like knitted tubing for hems, borders, and edging using double sided needles.

Backstitch: A straight line stitch along a selvage, often used to seam two pieces together. This stitch creates a fluid, circular motion as the needle is inserted under two rows, and then backwards one row, and so on.

Backstitch Seam: A seam stitch used to attach two pieces of a knitting project together by placing both with right sides facing each other, selvedge edges lined up, and working the needles in two rows forward and one row backward.

Backward Loop Cast: On A common and simple form of casting on that includes a slip knot and a chain of half stitches.

Bind Off Knit: Used to complete the finishing edge of a knitting project, it requires one to first knit each loop before passing it over the succeeding loop.

Bind Off Purl: Used to complete the finishing edge of a knitting project, it requires one to first purl each loop before passing it over the succeeding loop.

Blocking: Used to complete the finishing edge of a knitting project, it requires one to first purl each loop before passing it over the succeeding loop.

Blanket Stitch: Commonly used as an ornamental edge finish, it is a basic stitch of broadly spaced, interlocking loops or purls.

Bobble: The bobble stitch is a series of stitches in one specific spot that create a bump or ball-like decoration.

Brioche: A combination of tucked stitches (such as a yarn over or a slipped stitch) which form a ribbed pattern in knitting through a particular repetition of the stitches.

Cable Cast-On: A technique of casting on where a new loop is drawn through the two preceding loops and added to the needle creating a denser, corded edge.

Cables: A knitting pattern that involves crossing one group of stitches over another to create many different decorative patterns that resemble cables or cords.

Cast On: This is the groundwork that forms the base for your whole project. It establishes the first row of loops on the needle from which you will perform various stitches required for the chosen pattern.

Centered Double Decrease: A decorative stitch that results in a symmetrical pattern and requires three stitches where the center stitch is concealed by the stitch on either side of it.

Chain Stitch: A decorative stitch that resembles chain links in which each stitch forms a loop through the end of the succeeding stitch.

Continental Knitting: A style of knitting in which the yarn is held in the left hand, instead of the right.

Couching Stitch: Sometimes used as an outline to a design for greater dimension. It's a method in which a piece of yarn is placed on top of the knitted piece and fastened down with tiny stitches.

Cross-Stitch: A stitching technique in which pairs of diagonal knitting stitches of the same length cross each other in the middle to form a "cross" or "x" shaped pattern.

Daisy Stitch: A stitching technique used to make the petals of a flower. By bringing the needle up from the bottom of the project and back down in the same spot (which will become the center of the flower) leaving a tiny loop in the length of the desired petal, and finally securing the edge of the petal with a small stitch at the outer edge.

Double Cross-Stitch: Following the method of the cross-stitch, this stitch adds an additional two crossing stitches which result in an 8-pointed design.

Double Point Needles: Knitting needles with points on either end of needle instead of just on one end, these needles make circular knitting easier for projects such as socks.

Drop Stitch: This technique gives the knitting project a light and airy illusion by utilizing additional loops around the working needle. These elongated stitches create an appealing ribbed effect.

Duplicate Stitch: Process by which a stitch is duplicated on top of an existing stitch to add dimension or to emphasize a particular aspect of the knitting project.

English Knitting: As the opposite of Continental knitting, with English knitting, the yarn is held in the right hand and wrapped around the right needle before pulling the stitch through.

Couching Stitch: Sometimes used as an outline to a design for greater dimension. It's a method in which a piece of yarn is placed on top of the knitted piece and fastened down with tiny stitches.

Frogging: The process of unraveling, or pulling out stitches, to redo after a mistake.

Garter Stitch: An effect that is created when every row of the pattern is knitted. The result is a ridged piece that looks identical on both front and back.

Gauge: A unit of measurement counting the rows and stitches one needs in a square of the knitting project to be sure of the accurate size of the finished product.

I Cord: A thick, cord-like knitted tubing used for hat straps, purse handles or even closures, using double sided needles.

I Cord Bind-Off: The process of creating an attached i-cord as one is binding off, creating an appealing cording finished edge.

I Cord Cast-On: Giving the same corded finished edge as the I Cord Bind-Off, this process is created during the beginning of the project as one is casting on.

Intarsi: An artistic technique in which colored yarns are used to illustrate pictures and designs within the knitting project.

Joggles Join: The process of changing colors in one's knitting process seamlessly.

Kitchener Stitch (Graft): This stitch, also referred to as grafting, is a means to join two separate knitting pieces that have not yet been completely cast off, creating an invisible seam at the two edges.

Knit 2 Together: Method by which the right needle is inserted simultaneously into two stitches and treated as one single stitch. Used to decrease stitches.

Knit Stitch: The most basic stitch in the craft of knitting.

Knitted Cast-On: A simple method of casting on using the actual knit stitch to do so.

Lifted Increases: A method of subtly adding stitches, one stitch at a time, so the finished technique is nearly invisible.

Live Stitch: A stitch that has not yet been cast off.

Long-Tail Cast-On: A method of casting on in which one starts with a long tail of yarn and forms stitches that include the tail as well as the other side of the yarn.

Loop Cast-On: A method of casting on by forming loops and sliding them onto your needle. Often used when finishing buttonholes to cast on new stitches.

Magic Loop: The magic loop method is ideal for knitting socks or other knitting projects in the round with small circumferences. It is accomplished with a circular needle.

Make 1: A technique for increasing stitches, carried out between two existing knitted stitches.

Mattress Stitch Seam: A stitch used in the joining of two knitted pieces right along their edges in such a way that the seam is nearly invisible to the eye.

Overhand Seam: A very simple way to seam two knitted pieces together by placing them together with edges lined up and taking the threaded needle through both pieces close to the edge creating a winding seam down the outer edge of the joined parts

Pick Up and Knit: A process of picking up stitches on a finished knitted project to add edging, ribbing, and extended pieces, taking the needle and literally picking up a stitch at the edge to begin knitting new addition.

Provisional Cast-On: A manner of casting on in which the waste yarn used can then be pulled out permitting one to continue knitting in the opposite direction. This method creates a continual with no boundaries.

Purl 2 Together: A method to decrease stitches in which one purls two loops on the left needle resulting in the two stitches becoming one.

Purl Stitch: Along with the knit stitch, this is the most basic stitch in the craft of knitting and is essentially the exact opposite stitch of the knit stitch.

Reverse I Cord: Uses the same technique as the regular I-Cord, the difference being that the thread will be pulled up towards the front of the piece.

Reverse Shaping: The process of knitting a mirror image of another part of a knitting pattern as when you are making a cardigan sweater and the two front panels are the exact opposite shape of one another.

Reverse Single Crochet: Often referred to as the "crab stitch," this process requires one to crochet single stitches in the opposite direction of the common method. It produces a sturdier edging to projects and provides a decorative ridge along afghans and blankets, sweater necklines, and other pieces.

Ribbing: The intended outcome when one combines knit and purl stitches in the same row to create a stretch fabric ideal for sleeves and neck holes.

Running Stitch: A straight, over-and-under stitch which can run diagonally or horizontally and vertically over a knitted piece.

Satin Stitch: A series of flat stitches embroidered close together on top of a knitted project, used to make decorative designs and embellishments.

Selvage (Selvedge): A practice in which a reinforced edge is formed on a knitted project by alternating the stitch pattern at the start and finish of each row, creating a finished edge or one prepared for seaming.

# Chapter 4: Basic Knitting Techniques

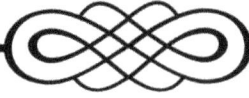

## Techniques for Holding Yarn

### 1. English Style

Knitting in English-style is achieved by keeping the yarn in your right hand. The patterns are formed on the piece's exterior (public-facing) face. Knitting English style (also known as' throwing') is characterized by holding the yarn in your right hand and wrapping it around the needle. The movement can be subtle or deliberate, and there are countless variations of how your right-hand holds the yarn. English knitting is a knitting style that includes keeping the thread, alongside the working needle, in the dominant hand. While it is popular in the British Isles and North America, knitting in English is done worldwide by knitters and is perhaps the most common. More than 60 percent said they knit English style in a survey of just under 300 all Free Knitting writers.

### 2. Continental Style

Continental knitting is accomplished by holding both the knitting and the purling yarn in your left hand. The patterns are formed on the piece's exterior (public-) face. Continental knitting (also known as' picking') is reputed to be easy. The yarn is kept in your left hand, and you don't need to move the thread at all once you get used to this form. Only pick the pin and get on with it. Continental knitting is a type of knitting, where the knitter keeps the yarn with the non-dominant side. Most knitters find this approach much faster, and crochets who are learning how to knit also find continental in their hands feel more normal. Approximately 30 percent of knitters from the above survey knit continental. As this style keeps the material in the hand that is not dominant, to switch between knitting and purling, it is unnecessary to transfer the thread either in the front or in the back of the needles. Instead, the yarn is either positioned in the non-dominant hand above or below the needle.

### Norwegian Knitting

The Norwegian knitting style is distinct due to the way purl stitches are handled. This particular hold places the working yarn in the non-dominant side, making it a continental variant; the knit stitches are worked much like the standard continental type.

### Russian Knitting

Russian knitting is very similar to standard continental knitting and the knit and purl stitches are worked in the same way themselves. The only difference with Russian knitting is that the working yarn is wrapped around the non-dominant hand's pointer finger, very similar to where it originates as the leading leg from the cloth. It makes a very close grip on the Russian style that helps you to flip the yarn over the tip of the needle instead of taking it with the needle itself. This technique is similar to kneading the lever with the yarn in the non-dominant hand.

## Portuguese/ Incan/ Turkish Style

By holding the yarn around the neck or from a hook in the necklace type, this method is done, enabling the knitter to knit on the opposite Usually, patterns are produced by stranding the yarn outside the piece. This knitting style is a real attention-getter— you tie the yarn to tension around your arm, and then just flip the working yarn to create stitches with your thumb. Purl stitches are usually quicker with this style, so it's perfect on the wrong side to work stockinette in the round. Portuguese knitting is a particularly great knitting keep since the yarn tension is not at all carried in the hands. Rather, Portuguese knitters tie the yarn around their necks. The rationale why numerous knitters like this style are because pace make the fingers frees up. The tension is kept in the hands in every different knitting style; this provides two things for the hands to do at the same time— keep the yarn and work the stitches with the needles. There's one less thing you have to think about when making the stitches when the stress is kept around the arm. This technique is also perfect for helping with knitting discomfort since the yarn retains so much of the tension in the hands. If you're not into out of the way to knit with the yarn around your arm, you can also purchase a Portuguese pin that added to your shirt and keeps the tightness there.

## Combination Knitting

Consider combination knitting if you are searching for ways to make your Continental knitting even quicker. To be more productive, the purl stitches are twisted the reverse way around, meaning the knit stitches are going around through the other loop.

## The Slip Knot

Nearly all cast-ons require a slip knot. If you do not know how to make a slip knot, taking a few minutes to master this simple knot will help you moving forward.

- -Make a loop in the yarn.
- -Hold the loop between your right forefinger and thumb, where the yarn crosses.
- -Make a second loop with your left hand.
- -Feed the second loop through the back of the first and pull taut.
- -Adjust your slip knot by pulling on the free end of the thread.

## Casting On

The first step to knitting is called "casting on". This is done by creating the first row of stitches on your needle. This is your foundation and will become one side of your scarf, so it is important to make it neatly. There are many methods of casting on. Some types are more suitable for specific projects, but the long-tail cast-on is most common. You will never go wrong by mastering the long-tail cast-on technique!

In the example above, we determined that the 6-inch scarf requires a total of 24 stitches for the width. Start by measuring a piece of yarn. Allow 1 to 2 inches for each stitch you will be casting on. If you are using a Bulky or Chunky yarn and big needles, you will need 2 inches per stitch (48 inches, or 4 feet). If you are using finer yarn and smaller needles, you will be fine with the 1-inch estimation. I usually add about 6 inches to my total, just to be safe.

Do not cut the yarn. Just hold it where you have measured your desired length.

Step One: Make a slip knot at the place where you have marked the length of your yarn for casting on. Slip the loop over one needle and pull the tail to tighten it.

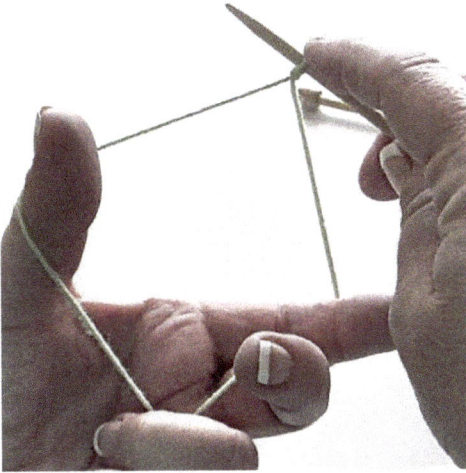

Step Two: Hold the needle in your right hand with your index finger on top, holding the slip knot in place.

Step Three: With your left hand under the needle, wrap one strand around your index finger and the other around your thumb. You should have a triangle shape with your needle at the top point and your two fingers making the two points for the triangle base.

Step Four: Bring the needle down so the yarn makes a "V" between your thumb and forefinger, which are now positioned like you are pointing a gun.

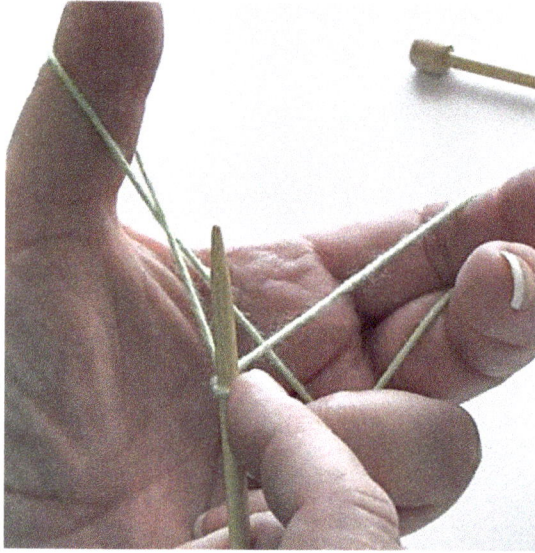

Step Five: With your right hand, guide the tip of the needle under the left side of the yarn that is looped around your thumb.

Step Six: Guide the needle UNDER this point and OVER the yarn on the right side of your thumb.

Step Seven: Move the tip of the needle OVER the left side of the yarn on your index finger.

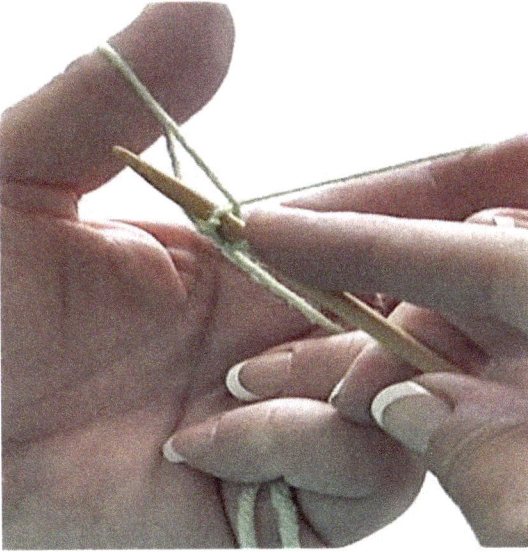

Step Eight: Swing the needle back THROUGH the loop on your thumb.

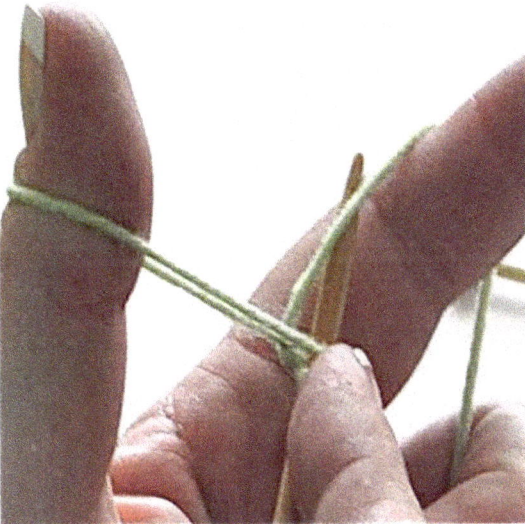

Step Nine: You will see that you have a loop on your needle now. Pull your needle up and release the yarn on your finger. Then pull the two yarn ends to tighten the casted on stitch.

Basically, the cast follows this pattern: under your thumb, over your index finger, and back through the thumb loop. Use this as your Cast-on Mantra: Under-Over-Through, Under-Over-Through….

Congratulations! You have your first stitch. Personally, I think casting on is the most complicated part of knitting a scarf. Once you master this, the rest will be easy.

## Knitted Cast On

Make a slip knot and leave it about an inch from the end of the needle. Slide your working/right needle into the slip knot from the left-hand front side and out through the right rear of the knot. Wrap the working yarn over the working needle counterclockwise (wrapping from the left over the needle to the right). Carefully tilt your working needle to pull it and the loop that you made back through the original stitch.

, you will gently slide the new stitch onto the left needle by placing the left needle on the right side of the stitch and pulling it off the right needle. In other words, the left needle needs to go into the stitch from the same direction as the right needle did. Repeat this process until you have the proper amount of stitches on the needle.

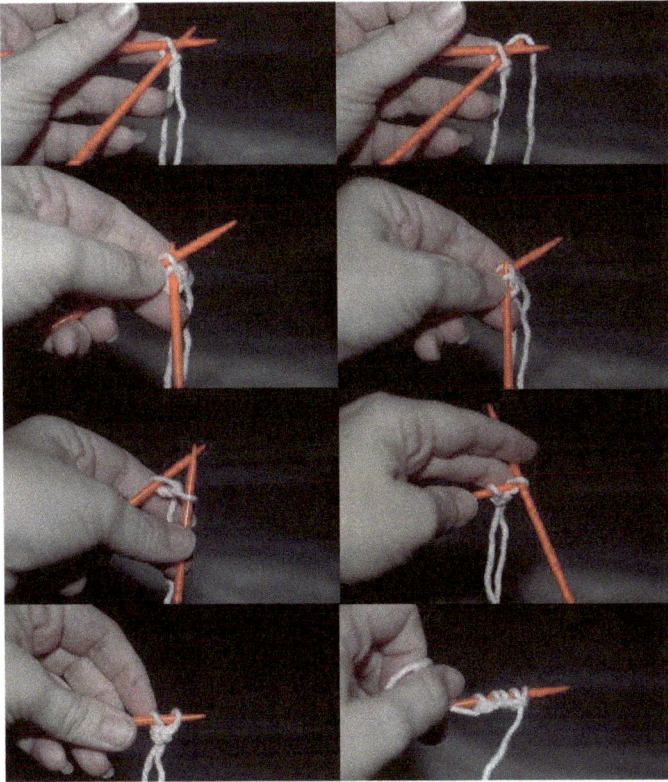

**Figure out How to Knit: The Long-Tail Cast-On**

Figure out how to weave a long-tail cast on making with this selective how to sew for tenderfoot's asset.

making a long tail (around 2- and one-half inch" to three" for each line to be thrown on), make a slipknot and spot on right needle.

Spot thumb and pointer of left hand between yarn closes with the goal that working yarn is around forefinger and the last part is around the thumb.

With your different fingers, secure the finishes a couple of crawls beneath the needles. Hold palm skywards, making a pattern V of a yarn.

Put the needle upward through the circle on the thumb, snatch the principal strand around pointer with the needle, and return down through circle on the thumb.

Drop circle off the thumb and, putting thumb back in V setup, tenderly fix coming about join on the needle.

Be certain not to cast-on too firmly or freely — join ought to effectively slide to and from on the needle without looking free and "loopy."

Fledgling Knitting Practice: Cast on 20 lines. Presently remove the entirety of the join from the needle (I know, I know…) and cast on 20 lines once more. Rehash this procedure until you feel extremely great with this cast-on. At the point when you are simply figuring out how to sew, it requires a significant stretch of time to get that muscle memory instilled, so keep at it! It'll come; I guarantee.

In the event that you are searching for help on the best way to begin knitting, this workshop is for you. With exercises intended for starting knitting needs, you'll get more than two hours of guidance covering lines, basic errors, and in any event, knitting in the round, yarn types and completing methods.

## Cable Cast-On

The cable cast-on begins like a knitted-on cast-on; however, after you make the first stitch, additional stitches are added between two stitches. The newly created stitch is moved to the left-hand needle and a new stitch made between this one and the preceding stitch. The cable cast-on creates a sturdy, reversible edge and is an acceptable replacement for either the long tail cast-on or the knitted-on cast-on if you prefer it.

# Chapter 5: Knitting Projects

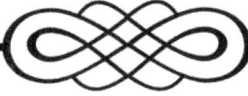

## Crimean Pelmet

It's a kind of hat, half-sided and convenient for people traveling by night, playwrights, and so on.

Dark wool and 4 frames, No. 8. No. 8. Cast 90 stitches on each pin and 30 stitches.

First-round — knitting basic. Then render 32 ribs, 3 square, 3 pearls.

Thirty-fourth — you're going to have 39 stitches on a hole. Hold the other 5 1, holding the ribs still even: 32 rows (and not rounds) back and forth, but add 15 stitches on each end of the last 2 sides.

Knit the stitches remaining on the 3rd column, take one stitch out of the 1 5 at the end of each side and knit it with the last stitch of each side. Repeat so before all 1 5 are obtained.

Now draw 27 stitches on each leg, knit 16 circles.

Cast down. Turn back.

**Muff.**

**Iron No. 13 sticks, and I oz. Rich Andalusian steel. For a 42-cast child; for a complete 60 cast.**

First side-spinning. succeeding lines.

Second row — knit I knit the second line in the following way: bring the wool around the needle as normal, except instead of pulling the thread around, let the wool hang directly over the left finger; wind the wool around your finger, place it on the needle again as though you were going to knit 'T; then do the same a third time, and finish working this item, whenever Continue to do the stitching and the succeeding simple in this manner.

Do 3 straight lines, then repeat from the is lane; be cautious in the alternating lines to create loops that do not have any in the preceding lines.

If the knitting is in inches, take off and stitch between top and bottom.

Create the muff as follows: either fill it with silk or knitting, for the latter cast 52 stitches into White Berlin to render it a little shorter with straight knitting than a loop- knitting. Break the two pieces together, with 3 or 4 wadding thicknesses between them. The rope should be sewn through the two holes and fastened off into an arc using an elastic run in.

To suit the above, Tippet or Victor in.

For a child, cast 36 stitches with a white Andalusian.

Knit, as in the preceding 18-inch design, and throw away; double and stitch the sides together.

Cut 2 wide white ornamental buttons and elastic throat fastening; add tiny tassels at the top.

Another approach to do this is to knit each stitch loop using Berlin wool with just a single thread.

Then wash the wool out, so it feels like the hair.

**Jacket sleeveless.**

**Pins No. 9, and fingering or black Berlin.**

Attach 98 stitches. Attach. Wear 12 circles. 12 circles.

13th row — knit 16, knit 30 wool over yarn, knit 6, cut wool, knit 30, knit 16.

The alternating lines are simple.

The fifteenth row — knit 17, knit 30 on yarn, knit 8, wool on, knit 30 on fur, knit 17.

17th row — 18 sweater, 30 knit fur, 10 knits, over, 30, knit, over, 18 knit wool.

Go for 60 rows in this direction.

On the other hand, remove 60 stitches on 33 rows back and forth.

Thirty-third row — 5 stitches tossed away (this must be at the beginning of the row); the remainder knit square.

Thirty-fourth row —the neck to 2 succeeding to the cast stitches at the end of the row. Reduce and cast off for the shoulder for 31 sets. So, put 16 stitches under the belt, then take the 66 under the pants on the bottom. Do 16 lines basic, then decrease by 38 lines for shoulder at the end of each part. Jump here for the face.

Then take the other arm off 16. On the other hand, take the remaining 60 stitches and make 32 rows on the other leg. Cast off 5 for the neck and then each for 32 rows at the end of each alternate

Sew on the arms.

Take up 53 stitches on the right hand and perform 2 straight lines. Create the buttonhole per 12 stitches; then knit the wool 3 times round the needle on the succeeding thread; knit the first component in the succeeding knead the second, knit the third part of this pattern.

Build three more rows and cast off.

Perform the same number of rows and sew buttons on the other foot. This is better to place a little piece of tissue beneath the base because the buttons are perfect for taking off.

Take the stitches of the waist; every 4 stitches.

Second row — increase, imitate to the middle, and again rise.

Repeat these six-row rises. Then growing in the middle 3 times. Do 4 more lines, and then 6 lines of the much coarser pin in brioche; do no increases now.

Cast down. Take back. Take the stitches around your arm, minimize by 5 times each alternating row for 4 rows, and create 4 rows with smaller sticks. Cast down. Take back.

This lightens the jacket to create violet or blue boundaries.

Crochet the ends on.

These are quite good, warm gifts for the needy, made of gross yarn. But, since the design is a tiny figure, there must be more stitching, particularly the tail.

## Children's Coat.

**Two bone pins, No. 14. (a fast pattern.)
It's the least elegant of the pair.**

Cast 20 stitches in Andalusian white and make 2 straight lines.

Third side — wool in front of the needle, the remainder smooth. Continue this row until 30 stitches have been inserted.

The thirteenth row — knitting simple. Perform 3 more straight lines.

17th row — knitted straight up to the last 2, knitted together.

Start to reduce until you just have 20 stitches.

Twenty-sixth row — the succeeding line straight at the end of this row added 9 additional stitches for the foot.

Twenty-eighth row — thread, the remainder white, before the needle. Repeat this row until 34 stitches are available. Perform 3 straight lines.

Thirty-seventh row — knit 18 rows, switch, and go now. To shape the foot, knit backward and forth on these 1 8 for 8 rods.

Forty-third rows — knit 18, then add 17 more lines, taking out the left pin — the stitches won't run down; those 17 should be opposite the stitches you let off. Perform 3 straight lines.

47th row — knit the last 2 at the toe together.

Reduce until you have just 31 in every row and cast off.

Take 17 loose stitches with steel pins and 22 more from the other side. No. 15, shaping the hip, making a total of 39.

The first row — knead 7, lift, knead 5. Repeat from.

The second row — you should have 44 stitches now. Wool knit 2 together before the needle. Pause. Repeat.

The third row — alternately knit and pearl for 12 sides.

Fifteenth row — pearl 2, 18 inches, knit 2.

Now make the second row of looping knitting (see Part I). This collection can be rendered in white or dyed fur, depending on your preference. A fun way to create a rosette tuft is to wind wool about 20 times around the forefinger, then push through the hole and draw up another piece of wool, cut the ends.

### Slipper.

Thick wool with 2 needles of wood. Appropriate are welfare or Allow thread and buttons No. 9.

Cast 15 stitches and knit 13 inches of thread.

Put on thirty additional stitches and knit eight sides.

Now each by knitting 2 at the start and 2 at the end of each alternating path. Knit 3 straight rows until just 1 8 stitches are remaining. Like before, decrease until 12 stitches remain. Knit 2 straight lines and throw off. It will be closely knitted to keep it solid.

Cut the end of the stripes on the side of the toe and knit an elastic border oval. Join the felt soils with the wool-colored wool braid and add them on the slippers. Attach a braid rosette in front,

### Infant's shirt.

**Put on 92 pins, and merino wool stitches No. 17.**

Knit 12 at the start and end of each side.

The sixty-eight interfering render four full four pearls alternating. Wear 102 rows and cast all but 12 stitches off. Knit the shoulder-strap 32 rods. Develop a second hand in the same way. For the gussets cast on 21, then at the end of each row, 2 knit together. Sew 20 points from the top of the jacket in the gusset.

Crochet an edge across the sleeves and top so; — I single) I link, miss 3, 2 tricycles, I link, 1 string, miss 3, I main, I cord, miss 3, 2 tricycles, I string, 2 tricycles in the same place Pause. Pause.

'The Vest of the Woman'. With a boy, too, is really sweet. Using Merino wool and No. 16 sticks. Pins No. 14 for a bigger scale.

*Beginning-Intermediate*

Cast-on using long-tail method 61 stitches.

Joining your circle: make sure all stitches are all facing the correct way. See casting on circular knitting in *the back*.

Using a stitch marker at the beginning will help you keep track of your starting point.

*Ribbing*

Using the chart below and or written instructions for a 1x1 rib. Work in this pattern for 2 inches. Note: when you are knitting in the round there is no working a (WS)Wrong Side row, only (RS)Right Side row.

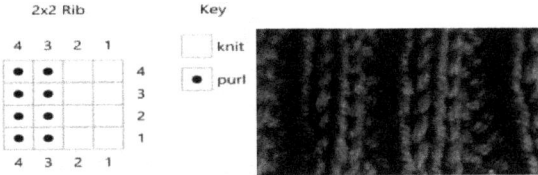

2x2 Rib    Key

knit

purl

**Written 2x2 Rib**

Rounds: K2, p2.

Main Portion of Hat:

Now that you have 2 inches of ribbing you can start working in stockinette stitch pattern for about 2 inches. Note: when you are knitting in the round there is no working a (WS)Wrong Side row, only (RS)Right Side row.

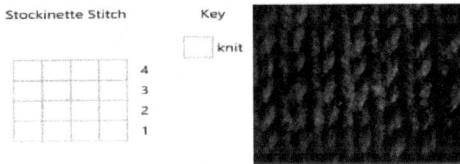

Stockinette Stitch    Key

knit

**Written Instructions: Stockinette Stitch**

Rounds: all rounds just use the knit stitch until you have 2 inches.

Decreasing for the Crown:

Using your stitch markers, divide the number stiches by 3.

Placing a stitch marker every 20 stitches. Follow the written instructions below:

Round 1: Knit 10, place stitch marker, knit 20, place stitch marker, knit 20, place stitch marker, knit the last 10. (60 stitches)

Round 2: Knit 8, k2tog, slip marker, ask, knit 18, k2tog, slip marker, ssk, knit 18, k2tog, slip marker, ssk, knit 8. (54 Stitches) (this is a decrease round and you will be decreasing 6 stitches)

Round 3: knit all stitches. Repeat rounds 2 and 3 until you have a total of 6 stitches left.

**Hat Closure**

Cutting the yarn leaving about 3 inches of yarn. Take a tapestry needle and us the needle to remove the stitches off the knitting needles. Pull yarn tight and sew in the left-over yarn. See Below.

**Simple Fingerless Gloves**

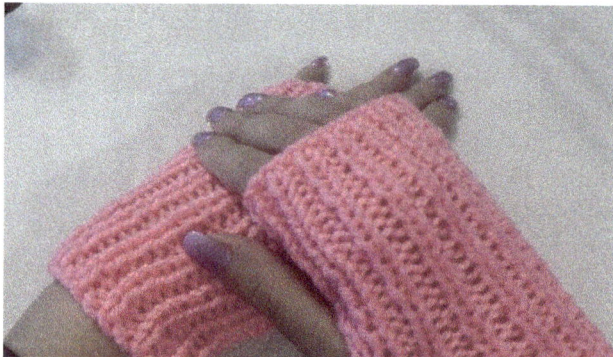

Materials

Knitting Needles size 7

Yarn: 1 Ball of your choice yarn weight 4 (worsted weight yarn)

Measuring Tape

Scissors

Tapestry Needle

Level: Beginner

Stitches you will need to know (these stitches can be found in the back):

Long-Tail Cast On

Knit

Purl

Simple Bind Off

Sizes for (Small, Medium, Large)

Small sizes will fit a range of people from children to young adult. You may have to adjust for the length of the gloves, but no the stitches required.

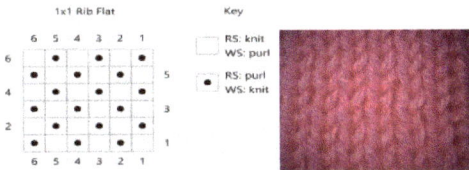

*Note reading the 1x1 Rib Flat chat (RS) Right Side rows – the odd rows are followed from right to left. The (WS) Wrong Side rows – even rows are followed from left to right.

Written 1x1 Rib Flat

Row 1 and all RS rows: (K, p) across all stitches.

Row 2 and all WS rows: (P, k) across all stitches.

Begin

Cast on using long-tail method (28, 38, 48) stitches. Working in the pattern above in either chart or written instructions for children for 5 inches in length and adults for 7 inches in length.

Once you have you have reached your desired length bind off and begin sewing up the two longest sides leaving a 1.5-inch opening for your thumbs.

## Chapter 6: Knitting Stitches

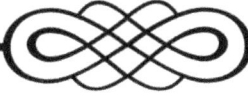

# Telling Knits and Purls Apart

It's important to be able to visually distinguish between a knit and a purl. A single knit stitch looks like a V, and a purl stitch looks like a little bump (or, a "pearl"). Take a moment to look at your work and see if you can pick out the knits and the purls.

When you're working some of the stitches below that require you to switch from knitting to purling, remember that each time you switch, you must move the yarn from behind the knitting needle (for knit stitches) to in front of the knitting needle (for purl stitches) or vice versa.

## More about the Garter Stitch

You've already learned about the garter stitch, which is just knitting every row. What would happen if you purled every row? It would still be a garter stitch, because a purl is just a backwards knit.

The garter stitch is the same on both sides of the project, so it's great for projects in which sides don't matter, like scarves and washcloths.

Other stitch combinations, however, look different on each side. Patterns for projects like shirts and hats, whose insides will look different from the outsides, refer to the sides as the "right side" (the outside or visible side) and the "wrong side" (the inside). The first stitch below produces a different effect on each side of the project.

**The Stockinette Stitch**

Many shirts and sweaters are knitted using the stockinette stitch. To make the stockinette stitch, alternate rows of knitting and purling. So, you'll knit every row on the right side, and you'll purl every row on the wrong side.

**The Rib Stitch**

The rib stitch creates a stretchy effect on a project. To make it, do two knit stitches, then two purl stitches, two knits, two purls, and so on in each row; and every time you switch to a new row make sure you are staying in line with the knits and purls of the preceding row.

**The Seed Stitch**

To create the seed stitch, alternate every stitch between a knit and a purl; and when you switch to a new row, make sure you're not in line with the knits and purls of the preceding row. The effect is a bumpy, dotted look, like "seeds."

**The Basket-weave Stitch**

To create the pretty basket-weave stitch, you'll knit four stitches, purl four, knit four, purl four, and so on—and keep that same alignment for four rows, then switch the alignment to begin with purling (purl, knit, purl, knit) for four rows, and so on.

## The Mini-basket-weave Stitch

For this stitch, simply cut the basket-weave stitch pattern in half: knit two, purl two, knit two, purl two; do this for two rows, and then reverse: purl two, knit two, purl two, knit two. It's also similar to the rib stitch, but the alignment of the knits and purls is purposefully broken.

In the upcoming we'll give you a more detailed pattern for making a mini-basket-weave stitch scarf.

Knit Stitch- In order to do this stitch, you need to have some stitches on your knitting needle already so go ahead and cast on 10 stitches. Holding the needle that has the cast on stitches on it in your left hand, and with your yarn to the back of your work take the needle in your right hand and insert it through the first loop on the needle in your left hand. You will insert the needle from the front of the stitch and slide it behind the needle in your left hand.

you want to wrap the working end of your yarn around the needle in your right hand working from right to left and going from back to front. You will then using the needle in your right hand bring the yarn you just wrapped, through the first stitch that is on the left needle and carefully slide the first stitch off or the needle in your left hand creating a new loop on the needle in your right hand.

You have created your first knit stitch. You should continue on using the same technique until you feel comfortable with this stitch.

One thing you need to remember while you practice this stitch is that you always want to keep the yarn behind your work.

Purl Stitch- Once again you will want to start with having some stitches already on your needle so cast on 10 stitches to learn the purl stitch. Hold the needle that has the cast on stitches in your left hand. With your yarn in front of your needle you will need to insert the needle in your right hand into the first loop on the needle in your left hand from back to front.

you will need to wrap the working end of your yarn around the needle in your right hand from right to left. Bring the needle in your right hand as well they yarn you just wrapped through the first loop on your needle in your left hand and slide the first stitch off of the needle in your left hand.

Now you have created your first purl stitch. You will continue to follow this technique until you are comfortable making a purl stitch. When creating a purl stitch, you need to remember to keep the working end of the yarn in front of the needle.

With these two stitches you will be able to create most patterns. For example, you can create a basket weave simply by using the knit stitch and the purl stitch. Here is how to do this.

Basket weave- You will want to cast on 8 stitches to start out with. On rows one and two you will purl stitch 2, knit stitch 4, purl stitch 4, knit stitch 4 and repeat for the width of the garment, finishing with 2 purl stitches. On the upcoming two rows you are going to do just the opposite, knit stitch 2, purl stitch 4, knit stitch 4, and purl stitch 4. You will continue this finishing up with a knit stitch of 2.

It is important to note right here that you will only use the sets of two stitches when you begin a row and end a row. Do not repeat the sets of two throughout the pattern unless it is at the beginning or end of a row. For example:

o=purl stitch, x= knit stitch

Row 1- ooxxxxoooxxxxoo

Row 2- ooxxxxoooxxxxoo

Row 3- xxooooxxxxoooxx

Row 4- xxooooxxxxoooxx

Do you see how the start and the end of each row have sets of two and in the rows, we have sets of 4? This is the type of pattern you will want to do for the width of your project.

You will continue following this patter until you reach the end of your stitches so for 8 stitches it would be row 1, row 2, row 3, row 4, row 1, row 2, row 3, row 4. As you can see if you want to make a larger project you need to make sure you cast on in multiples of4 otherwise your weave will not come out correctly.

If you followed a long with this pattern you will see that you have created an entirely different pattern simply by using two basic stitches. Of course, not all of the stitches are this easy but several of them are.

At this point you will want to work with the stitches you have learned and start a project. I always suggest that you work an entire project with each stitch that you learned. For example, try making a blanket with the knitting stitch, try making a scarf with the purl stitch and work your magic with a basket weave stitch on another project of your choice.

I suggest this because this will allow you to get used to using that stitch, it builds up the muscle memory in your hands and it allows you to become familiar with each stitch.

This way when a pattern calls for a purl stitch you know exactly what you need to do instead of having to waste your time looking up each stitch one at a time.

It can be a little bit difficult at first and sometimes frustrating but when you take the time to build muscle memory by practicing the stitches and take the time to learn each stitch one by one, knitting becomes a lot more fun and a lot easier especially for beginners.

we are going to learn about increasing and decreasing your stitches and how to create your own projects and finish up the readings with some simple tips and tricks for beginning knitters.

## Chapter 7: Knitting Patterns

# Garter Stitch Scarf

The scarf pattern is perfect when you are a beginner. It requires only one thread-and it is a perfect way to apply simple knitting skills. You need to be able to cast off your knitting, finish knitting stitches, and cast off your knitting to complete this scarf.

This scarf was knitted with Panda Heath, an 8-ply yarn, on oversize needles (6.00mms), resulting in a perfectly soft yet lightweight scarf. Panda Heath discontinued some years ago, but you can replace any eight-ply wool, and the pattern still works.

This scarf is approximately 200 cm long, with its fringes and 22 cm wide, in its resting state.

A pattern will usually indicate the number of balls you would use for creating the piece. In my scarves, I used pure wool and took about 4 to 5 50 grams of wool, but the number of balls needed depends on the yarn that you choose.

You will need a couple of 6.00 mm single pointed needles to knit these Garter Stitch Scarf patterns (or the size needed to give you the appropriate tension).

Tension

The tension for this scarf stitch is 22 stitches, and the 10 cm square is 26 rows.

Put on 34 stitches with knitting instructions.

Round 1: * Knit.

Repeat 1st row until your job is 180 cm long (or desired length).

Cast off.

Finishing your scarf- If you are satisfied with your scarf, you can also add a fringe if you want to add a special touch.

For the Simple Fringe:

Cut 48 bits of yarn approximately 12 cm long.

Take three yarn strands for a part of the fringe and fold in half to help form a loop. Draw the loop through your knitted scarf fabric and then draw the ends through the loop with a crochet needle.

Push the knot of the fringe firmly.

Eight ties between the two ends of your scarf evenly, and you are done!

For a fringe knotted: this is achieved by cutting yarn bits about 20 cm long.

Take four strands of yarn and fold them in half to form a loop to create a portion of the fringe. Draw the loop through your sharp fabric with a crochet hook and then draw the ends through the loop.

Push the knot of the fringe close.

Five knots are identical around the end of your scarf, leaving space for a knot at either end. At each end, two strands (instead of four) form a marginal knot.

Once you add all your knots to the scarf, you may tie them. Divide each border knot (except the two border knots) into two, tie a knot halfway down the border by using four bands from one border knot, and four bands from the upcoming knot line. Keep operating in this way until all the fringes of the middle are together.

Then join the four strands of the end knot on the remaining four strands of the border knots to finish the line.

## Stockinette Stitch Scarf

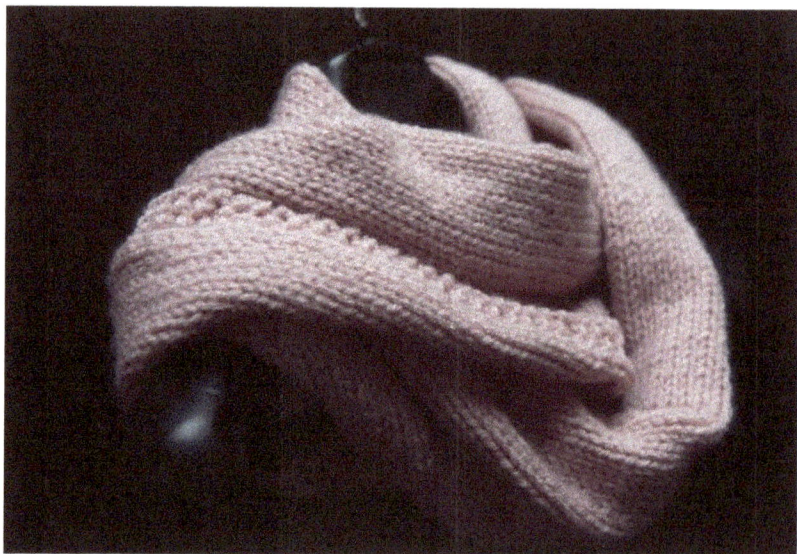

Everywhere you can find the stockinette stitch: scarves, shoes, sweaters, blankets, hats, etc.

To integrate the stitch into your knitting repertoire, pay attention to the following: if the stitch of the stockinette is right or wrong (though both sides may, of course, be "right" according to the intended design). Usually, the right side is the smooth side, knit, or stockinette. The stitches look small on this side. The bumpy side of the punching fabric is known as reverse stockinet or purl.

The lining of the Stockinette coils on the bottom. The top and bottom (horizontal) borders are bent to the front or smooth side. The edges of the surface fall to the bumpy side.

Sweater designers also purposely use this rolling feature to create rolled joints or cuffs, and you can create simple strings or straps simply by knitting in the stitch of a very narrow (say, 4 or 6 stitches across) band.

You have to overcome this pattern by working the three or four stitches of the edge in some flat stitch (such as grit or seed stitch) if you want to lie flat.

When working on a stitch of stockinet and lose track of how you knitted or purled the last row, look at your knitting. Keep your needles ready to knit (with the LH needle carrying the stitches) and look at what faces you. If you look at the (smooth) side of your knitting, you knit. You purl if you look at the (bumpy) hand of the purl.

When working the storage stitch in the ring, you see the cast and curl the edges off. In some designs, this is often used as a custom design feature, but sometimes we do not like the look, like when knitting an afghan scarf or square.

## Reasons

The reason why its curls are related to the stitch structure itself. Because of the inherent variations between the knit stitch and the purl stitch, the stockinette curls. Knit stitches are much shorter than purl stitches and narrower.

If you work in style with knits and puree lines on both sides, this stitch discrepancy does not matter but working in stockinette stitches where all knit stitches are on one side, and the knitting tends to curl.

## Prevention

If you have not yet built the project that you want but do not want to curl, the most common method for reducing or avoiding curl is by using a border stitch knit in a different stitch pattern while the rest of the project is knit.

Many heavy knitting patterns have a curling edge, moose stitch, stitch, or a similar pattern that contains relatively evenly knitted and purled patterns that helps to balance lines to limit curling.

At the beginning and the end, you would possibly up to six stitches on each side and five or six rows to avoid curling. On socks and hats, this means to knit in a ribbing or a non-curling pattern at least one inch per 2 1/2 cm before going on to stockinet.

Another way is to knit stockinet in the round. The edges that are cast and bound still curl, but you can knit a scarf around; for example, add tassels to the ends to hold the edges flat.

## Fixing curled knitting

What if you knit a project already and do not like the curling?

There are a variety of solutions that work better than others. Some people tell you that blocking helps to smoothen out stores and sometimes it, at least briefly, but it is not a secure remedy, and it is not going to last.

However, as you can expect, this greatly changes the look and feel of the yarn, so check a swatch to make sure you are satisfied with the results before using the full product.

You may add a crocheted border around the border, but like knitting on the border it must be fairly large, and it might not be a good result (if you knit a scarf as big as you like and do not want to add a couple of inches on either side).

Other choices include purposely dropping stitches that open up the fabric and lace it, dropping stitches, converting the scarf to ribbing instead of storage, and lining it with fabric that keeps it in place. Finally, you can only call it an aspect of design and live with the curl.

## Fleck Stitch Envelope Purse

Fleck stitch is a simple knitting stitch that involves a row of ribbing to a storage stitch area. This form of knitting pattern is used to make small bags.

For people who are new to knitting, it is a good idea to begin working with something small and flat, because these items do not need many forms. For example, they can make a bag with a fleck stitch. This small bag is easier to make and easier to use. It is thin, rectangular, folded, and sewn together, making it knit very quickly.

Materials used for the knitting include cotton wool yarn or medium weight cotton (approx. 140 yards), one pair of US knitting needles (size 8), scissors, yarn needles, and an I-cord creator (size 8).

You can start knitting the bag after preparing the necessary materials. Paint the first series of 35 stitches using single-pointed needles. Then knit for 20 inches in fleck stitch (underneath) and tie the last rows together.

You will fold it in a rectangular shape to overlap 8 inches with a 4-inch flap at the end. The lateral seams must be sewn with a mattress stitch or with a seaming tool.

Cast 4 stitches and produce 30 inches of I-cord using double-pointed needles.

The I-cord strap can also be made quicker by using an I-cord printer.

Sew the handle to the inside of the case.

**Leg Warmers**

Step 1:

The Things you need Yarn, of course, knitting needles, the ones with the cord between them.

I use Rico wild wool in color number 015 and knitting needles in diameter 8 mm, I assume that it is US 11.

Two yarn skeins (200 g) should be appropriate.

Step 2: I start with the hat; I cast five stitches first.

Step 3: First round

The first round is a little difficult; the stitches, as seen in the picture, have to be spread and all stitches twice. As seen here, you can do this or by working on the front and back of a thread. Once you finish knitting the first two stitches, you will place the stitches on the needles, etc.

Once the round is completed, using a small yarn loop in another color to mark the beginning of the round.

Step 4: Add round in the round, you have to add five stitches each, to achieve the floral shape like hat shape on a regular basis.

In the second round, each second stitch is twice as big in the third round and so on. The remainder of the stitches is knitted, and markers are used to support you.

I stopped at 23 frames; if you like, you might make it bigger.

Step 5: Decrease of stitches

You have to start decreasing stitches when you have reached the desired size by knitting two stitches as one. Make sure for every round, you decrease every fifth stitch

Step 6: Edge

Now knit a few rounds to the edge without any increase or decrease. I had six rounds alternating with a purl stitch and a knit stitch.

To end the hat, make sure you do not do it to the company.

Step 7: Limit Achieved!

So here you finish your hat, cover in the fabric the ends of the yarn, and it is ready to wear.

Step 8: Leg warmers

To create the leg warmers, you need to cast on 36 stitches and then knit four rounds of two stitches alternating of two knit stitches.

Then, starting with a knit stitch, then alternating two knit stitches and 2 pure stitches, then two lines starting with the two cut stitches and then alternating 2 pure stitches and two knit stitches, proceed with this pattern till you have the desired length.

The pattern (; x = knit stitch, o = purl stitch) will look like this: Step 9: The Wrist Warmer Handle warmers are identical to those used to make the leg warmer, except they only have 24 stitches.

For the thumb hole, at the end of the sixth round, you can just flip over your work, knit back again, knit back and flip back and flip over and knit again as before.

## Chapter 8: Tips and Tricks

## Purchase Cheap, Plain Yarn

It's anything but difficult to be enticed by all the quiet, remarkable, delicate yarns out there. However, in all actuality, the main couple of things you weave won't merit the decent yarn. Additionally, it's gentler on your wallet to begin modestly and afterward move onto the sumptuous stuff when you realize you can do it some equity.

I don't get my meaning to plain yarn? no fuzzy yarn, no cumbersome yarn. You can discover the data on the yarn name itself;

the fiber substance will peruse "100% acrylic" or something comparative, and a small image of a yarn ball ought to have the number 4 on it, which implies that the yarn is worsted weight or medium weight. This is the most well-known yarn weight. Red Heart Super Saver yarn in your preferred shading is an extraordinary, modest, simple spot to begin.

### Deliberately Buy Your Needles

Needles aren't care for yarn where you can go through them. Your needles need to help you through the entirety of your future undertakings, and hence ought to be tough and agreeable. In a perfect world, you could go to your neighborhood yarn store and solicit to grasp a couple of sets from needles before choosing the brand and material you like, however, if you don't approach anything like that, we prescribe size 8 single-pointed bamboo needles.

My own needle inclination is aluminum since I like it when the yarn can undoubtedly sneak off of the needles; however that is an unsafe area to be in when you're a tenderfoot, and you're dropping lines like hotcakes.

Here's the key: when you've chosen whether or not you like this pair of size 8 bamboo needles (ideally in the wake of knitting your first swatch), and you've concluded that you like knitting and need to continue onward, spring for an exchangeable needle set. These sets are a lot of needle tips with strings that interface them. In fact, they are on the whole round needles, yet an enjoyment tip I learned at an early stage in my knitting vocation is that you can sew level on roundabout needles! Numerous individuals discover them simpler to hold than single-pointed needles, too. Pick a lot of exchangeable bamboo needles on the off chance that you preferred your first pair or aluminum if you didn't. Presently, you'll have each knitting needle size under the sun to play within your future undertakings, and you'll just need to stress over double pointed needles... in any case, we won't get into that now.

## Figure out how to Knit Continental Style

In case you're figuring out how to weave in current America, you're regularly learning one of two styles out of many: English or Continental. Actually, I learned English style: right now, hold your yarn in your right hand as you weave, and respite to fold it over your working needle each join.

With Continental style, on the other hand, you hold the yarn in your left hand and "scoop" at it with your correct needle. If any crocheters are perusing this reading, this may sound recognizable, and it's actual: it's regularly simpler for crocheters to figure out how to sew Continental style instead of English.

For what reason do I prescribe you figure out how to weave Continental? Mainland style is quicker and (ostensibly) simpler on your joints. On the off chance that you've just figured out how to sew English style, that is fine, and you can either change it up and figure out how to weave Continental or simply keep joyfully knitting English style. There's no standard here. However, I wish I'd figured out how to weave Continental style, since now I experience difficulty learning any style of knitting other than English, and I'm a genuine dawdler with regards to my knitting.

## Get familiar with the Knit Cast On

Numerous educators start with showing their understudies how to cast on with the substantially more-regularly utilized longtail cast on strategy. We do prescribe giving a shot the longtail cast-on technique before all else, yet if you think that its equitable confounds and baffles you, take a stab at learning the sew cast on strategy!

This is the cast on technique I for one learned with and keeping in mind that I never use it any longer; it was madly helpful to me to start with. While this cast on strategy isn't typically explicitly called for in an example (however can surely be utilized if no other technique is explicitly required), it's less difficult to get the hang of and shows you both how to cast on and how to finish a sew fasten in one. This may not sound good to you yet, yet after you've cast on and you begin figuring out how to sew a line, you'll see that you've just figured out how to do this, short one little advance.

**Start with a Swatch**

Presently, you have your yarn, needles, and a terrific thought of the absolute first scarf you'll sew. However, I'm here to hold up the "yield" sign in your face and suggest that you start off somewhat littler. As opposed to hopping directly into a scarf, weave up a swatch instead: that is, the point at which you figure out how to cast on and sew, simply sew a little square of texture in tie join (psst... strap fasten is basically knitting each join)! Along these lines, you can address any issues you experience without stressing over demolishing a dazzling scarf or paradise restrict, a present for a companion.

I bounced straight into a scarf myself, and I don't wear it right up 'til the present time because the start is simply so repulsive.

**Your Tension Will Be Terrible... Disregard It**

Knitting pressure is something even prepared knitters (such as myself!) battle with right up 'til today, however not exactly to a similar greatness as starting knitters. You'll see that your columns are definitely lopsided, your lines appear to hang at the edges, and your swatch looks more like a bit of work than an example of texture.

Imprint my words: you will develop out of this. Resemble Dory from Finding Nemo and simply continue swimming... err, knitting. Continue taking a shot at your swatch and keep on knitting ahead until you see your lines begin to try and up. Figuring out how to try and up your pressure really boils down to seeing how firmly you ought to wrap your yarn, which is something you can just learn through inclination and rehearsing. Hell, you may even find that you're never again including or subtracting irregular fastens any longer when you've sewed up a couple of inches!

Talking about... look at these instructional exercises for fixing pressure issues and forestalling paddling out!

The most effective method to Fix Tension Problems How to Prevent Rowing Out

## Utilize Basic Math

Recollect what number of lines you cast on with. Each line for the initial thirty lines or with the goal that you weave, tally what number of circles are on your needle when you've wrapped up. If you appear to have picked up or lost a join, something turned out badly. Try not to freeze! It's alright and totally typical for learners to wind up with more or less join than when they began. This sort of thing isn't generally worthy in a completed task. However, that is the reason we began with a swatch rather than a scarf!

on in your knitting profession, you can figure out how to recognize these knitting botches and right them, so it never seems as though you committed an error in any case. This implies getting dropped lines or thinking (knitting in reverse) to discover where you unintentionally included a fasten. Until further notice, you should just be centered around knitting each line gradually and cautiously and ensuring no increments or subtractions have happened. On the off chance that a join sneaks off of your needle, get it as fast as conceivable before it starts disentangling, and stick your needle back through the circle. You'll know whether you sew the fasten as of now if your yarn is coming out of it, or coming out of a join to one side of it; if the yarn is coming out of the line before it (to one side), you have not sewed that line yet.

Things being what they are, what do you do if you wind up with an excessive number of join and couldn't recognize your concern as it happened? In case you're feeling sufficiently sure to have a go at something past the weave fasten, presently is an incredible time to learn K2tog (sew two joins together). As opposed to place your needle into only the following fasten, continue jabbing until it likewise experiences the join to one side of it.

Imagine a scenario in which you have too not many joins. Attempt the M1 technique. Sew to around the center of your work. Do you see an even bar of yarn associating the line on your correct needle to the line to your left side? This is known as the stepping stool. Gather up the stepping stool with your left needle. It will make a kind of pseudo-circle to your left side needle. Treat that circle like some other fasten and sew it with your correct needle. You've quite recently expanded a line!

Try not to go Onto the Purl Stitch Prior in Mastering the Knit Stitch

Similarly, as you shouldn't attempt these simple, restorative increment and abatement techniques until you're completely sure that you could finish the sew line with your eyes shut, don't move onto the purl line until you're appropriately arranged. Hell, you could even weave up a whole scarf in tie join before moving onto the purl line just to be extra certain that you're prepared for that subsequent stage. You may even be prepared to attempt the purl line after only a couple of lines of the sew line. Everyone adapts in an unexpected way. All things considered, you would prefer not to confound yourself by moving onto another procedure and end up befuddling weave and purl down the line.

This was a misstep of mine. I attempted stockinette join first before consigning myself to the fastener line. Stockinette fastens; if you don't have the foggiest idea, is the place you weave one line and purl the other line. I had irregular squares of supporter line in my swatch since I would begin knitting as opposed to purling, or the other way around, unintentionally. Also, the entirety of the openings in my work since I would neglect to move the yarn either in reverse or advance before working the following fasten! There's an excess of potential for things to get untidy in case you're not 100% moving and grooving with the sew line yet.

### Recordings Are Your Best Friend

In case you're not in a position where you can be instructed face to face by another knitter or your family is resting thus you can't play a video showing you how to sew, hold on to learn until both of these are conceivable. Of course, pictures can be useful; however, knitting is such a movement-based specialty that it's critical to the point that you can dissect the moment developments in your educator's hands and gain from that.

Try not to try and waste time with instructional exercises that offer just composed directions. These will be simpler to follow and overly accommodating once you as of now have the nuts and bolts under control; however you won't see any of the wording or have the option to convert into solid activities the theoretical directions you're accepting.

## Chapter 9: Frequently Asked Questions

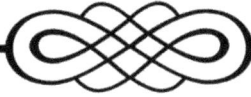

Why is knitting a good skill to have? Knitting is a brilliantly useful skill that can help you create a wide variety of your own products – everything from toys to clothing. But, not only that, it's scientifically proven to improve your mood, mind and body. It's a therapeutic skill which you will not regret learning!

How do you read a knitting chart?

The best way to read a knitting chart is in detail in this guide, in the Knitting Charts.

What I need to buy to start off knitting?

The Supplies of this guide gives you the basics of what you need to start knitting. However, the yarns, needles and anything extra you'll need for a specific pattern will be listed as one of the first pieces of information.

How do you do double-pointed knitting?

Double pointed needles are generally used for knitting in the round on projects that are too small for circular needles. They are often purchased in sets of 5. Here is a brilliant guide for how to use them, with these main top tips:

- Cast on to 1 double pointed needle.
- Then slip ½ the stitches onto another needle.
- Then a third onto another.
- Use a fourth needle to knit.

Does it cost a lot to knit?

Knitting can be done very cheaply if you know the right places to look. Local haberdashery stores will sell a wide range of products from high quality to budget, so it really is a skill that applies to everyone.

What is an easy way to learn how to knit?

The step-by-step guides provided in the Stitches of this guide will get you started.

How do you knit with 3 needles?

You will often use 3 or more needles when working with double pointed needles.

What are the differences for English and continental methods for knitting?

Everyone has their own preference when it comes to knitting style. You will eventually develop your own.

- English Knitting o Hold yarn in right hand to throw yarn when wrapping or easier with chunky weight yarns
- Continental Knitting o Hold yarn in left hand to pick the yarn when wrapping o faster when you're knitting the knit stitch o Alternating stitches is easier to Easier for crochets to learn

**What is knitting in tandem?**

Tandem knitting is a technique for knitting socks or gloves or anything in the round that comes in pairs and uses 9 DPNs; it casts on for both items in the pair at the same time, and involves completing a portion of one of the pair, then the same portion of the other item of the pair.

### Is it hard to knit a scarf?

In the Patterns of this guide, you will find a pattern for a knitted scarf designed specifically for novices. Scarves can be made by anyone at any skill level. If you're an advanced knitter, your creations can be much more complex and embellished.

### Is crocheting harder than knitting?

Crocheting is a different skill to knitting in the way that it uses one hook rather than two needles. Different people prefer different skills so practicing both is the best way to figure out which one you personally find easier and more suitable.

### Where can I find some great knitting patterns?

Knitting patterns can be found in haberdashery stores, but they are also available in abundance online. Just type 'Knitting Patterns' into any search engine and you will be spoilt for choice

### What are the succeeding steps once you've worked through this guide?

This reading gives you all the basics you need for starting knitting. Once you have gotten to grips with all of the stitches and patterns provided, it is time to move on to more complex patterns – you can maybe even create your own! Once you have mastered this skill, the possibilities are endless

# Chapter 10: Common Mistakes

You may ask, "Are there knitting mistakes?" Of course, there are mistakes everywhere and, in all things, especially in knitting, which could be very frustrating and confusing at the beginning. But these mistakes are easy to fix because if you can't correct them, you may not be able to proceed with your knitting projects.

Now, there are some effective fixing methods; you need to know that can help you to get out of any knotty situation you find yourself while knitting. Let us recall some of the common mistake's beginners make and how they can fix them using some proven strategies.

## A. When Some of Your Knitting is Loose, and Others are Tight

You may experience this mistake if you are not holding the tension of your working yarn consistently. In fact, the structure of the knit work will become messy and uneven. This will cause the knit stitches to be loose, and others will be tight too.

One of the best ways to resolve this issue is to look for a consistent and comfortable way of holding the yarn. If you can block and wash your knitting that alone can assist in correcting the problem, although, beginners can improve on this mistake through consistent practice.

## B. If the Yarn is Connected to the Second Stitch on the Row While You are Starting a New Row

The main reason for this mistake is that the yarn slipped off while you were stitching the preceding row. That means you were not able to pull through and create a new stitch. Therefore, you should turn the material in a way; it will appear as if you are concluding the last row. Then, slip the last stitch back onto the left needle and repeat the process. After this, you can turn the cloth and begin from a new row as the case may be.

## C. Dropping the Stitch

A mistake could happen if you just dropped the stitch. Now, to correct the error, you must pinch under the stitch to prevent it from disentanglement. Take the stitch back up as you insert the edge of the needle at your left hand. This action will enable you to place the dropped stitch at the front.

Additionally, you will see a loose thread on the stitch if it has already been untangled.

Then, you should knit the loose strand again when you want to put back the dropped stitch on the needle. However, you can handle this project easily by using a crochet hook and being careful not to overstretch the cloth too much as it can cause more damage to the material.

### Ways to Pick Up a Drop Stitch

There are various steps you can follow and pick up a drop stitch such as by inserting the crochet hook into the dropped stitch from the front. But you should ensure that the thread is placed at the back of the stitch.

Secondly, you should hold the strand of the ladder and pull it back from the stitch all the way to the front. After this stage, you should repeat all the steps above until you have knit back all the threads of the ladder. Finally, you can place it on the left-hand needle.

On the other hand, if you want to pick up a dropped purl stitch, you should follow the steps above and attach the hook from behind. My advice is that you should spend some time and understand how to correct dropped stitches since you may be making a mistake very often.

**D. Holes in Your Knit Work If there are holes in your knit work, you should know that there are reasons why that happened and try to fix it immediately. Some of the causes of holes in your project could be as a result of an extra wrap on the fabric or an unintentional yarn over on the needle.**

This could have occurred if the thread is in front while you attempted knitting a stitch.

It will inadvertently create a massive hole in the fabric.

However, ensuring that the yarn is in the back while knitting a stitch is essential, to prevent an unintentional yarn over.

Additionally, if you want to purl a stitch, endeavor to put the thread in front of the stitching.

Remove the mistaken knit stitch and tear open the yarn over, before continuing your knit work and then, fix the errors in that process.

Another way you can create holes in your knitting project is by raising the bar between two stitches and knitting into it, thereby making a mistake of an m1increase. In this case, you will notice that you are knitting in front of the stitch and this could cause a big hole in the knit work.

An excellent way to mitigate this lapse is by knitting into the back loop and reducing the size of the hole whenever you make an m1 increase.

Moreover, if you pick up any work mid-row and begin again from the wrong direction, you will make knitting mistakes.

Therefore, you should avoid placing your knitting mid-row and ensure handling the rows thoroughly in one sitting as you conclude the project. This will make it subtle and neat.

But you may ask, "Can I conclude the rows in one sitting?" Of course, you know, this is not achievable. Anyway, always ensure you attach the working yarn to the last stitch on the right needle, if you pick up your knit work after placing it mid-row.

# Conclusion

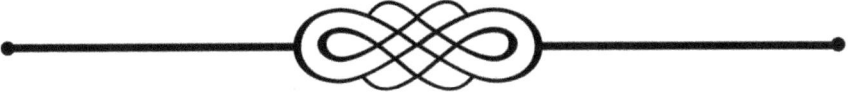

Thank you for making it to the end. Despite the fact that you might need to hop directly in there and begin utilizing a knitting pattern it is a smart thought to make a check swatch. Try not to skirt this progression, you will be grieved, and it's not justified, despite any potential benefits. A large portion of a line in one inch can wind up having a major effect to the general size of a sweater. Continuously weave the swatch in the join that you will utilize. Clearly different knitting patterns end up with different sizes so this issue. I generally attempt to make my swatch sufficiently large to make it a decent test. I generally go for at any rate 4" x 4". Encompass the swatch with a couple of columns of seed fasten knitting (weave or purl the contrary line of what you see confronting you on odd number lines). Start and end each line with four seed lines also. This join lies exceptionally level and will assist you with estimating precisely.

Needle size is substantially less significant than strain with a knitting pattern. A few people are free with their knitting pattern while others are tight. You can purposely adjust you pressure to make a different knitting pattern look. Free for a light open feel and more tightly for a hotter vibe. The more tightly weave may feel stiffer while the looser knitting piece may feel milder.

At the point when you have completed the swatch let it sit for a spell. The yarn needs to unwind and level out any difficult situations. Presently check the fastens and measure the columns per inch with a material tape. Make sure to attempt an estimation in a couple of different spots. Another route is to simply ascertain how enormous the all-out knitting pattern swatch ought to be. If 16 joins were thrown on for the and the check is 4th=1" the swatch should quantify 4" (don't gauge the seed fastens on each end). If you are excessively enormous, attempt needles that are a size littler. Or then again if you are excessively little, attempt bigger needles. Presently you have completed you can begin your knitting pattern with certainty realizing that the result of your works will really fit you!

I believe you have had a nice time going through all this. Knitting is a great hobby/occupation. As you begin your knitting journey, you will realize that your knitting is lose and sloppy, not to worry though because you will get better with time. All you need to do is to practice, practice, and practice some more until you become a guru at knitting.

If you are chasing a pattern or two, you will find that there are plenty of free ones online and if you require a little extra tuition to improve your knitting techniques you might also like to browse YouTube for additional knitting tutorials.

Now you know what you're doing and what you need to do to get started and continue. It's all about practice, and you need to take a break every now and again. Stretch your fingers, as it'll help to make sure that you don't' make simple mistakes that will cause you to get frustrated and put knitting down. Knitting may be a hobby, but it's one that does take time.

Never give up and try to unravel anything that's been dropped if you're having too much of a hard time. With these simple and easy patterns, you're practicing everything you need to know to go into more complex patterns to make perfect gifts and a way to spend a lazy afternoon.

If things are not going to plan, even after having studied this electronic reading material again, simply keep your patience and in a matter of weeks you could be knitting bonnets, scarfs and jumpers.

Knitting has also been recognized as a great form of past time as well as being an outstanding outlet for creative gift of talent. Knitting extremely easy and well occupation as your knitting can be done almost anywhere around with you, from your favorite place to the outside or even to school for a little fun knitting in your lunch break.

Arm knitting is quick, both to learn and to perform. You will get hours of pleasure from creating these radical patterns that offer you a mostly doable alternative to the traditional needles and yarn type weaving. You will enjoy this experience, and as you get more and more comfortable with this technique, you will find your creativity growing as well.

Invest the time necessary to learn how to arm knit, and you can then set about adding spice and variety to your wardrobe. You can even make your own gifts for friends and loved ones, or maybe, just maybe, you can turn this into a business.

Whatever your reasons for taking on arm knitting, the rewards of this new skill are many. Yes, there is a quick turnaround time for arm knitting projects, but you will get hours and hours of satisfaction from really putting your hands into it!

People knit for various reasons beyond just making clothes and knitting items for their family and friends. Some people knit to relax and de-stress themselves after a very stressful day, some people knit so they can quit smoking, and some people knit just so they can keep their hands busy while lazily watching television.

A lot of people love knitting because they get an immense satisfaction from turning a simple yarn into something more complex like a garment or a Christmas tree decoration. They love the process of turning something simple into something more useful. Knitting is also very relaxing. The repetitive movements, the rhythmic movements, as well as the mental focus one needs is some sort of meditation that helps ease the mind of anyone who knits.

A ball of yarn, no matter how beautiful the style or how lovely the color, is nothing until you are able to give it shape and purpose. The reason why knitting is so fulfilling is because when you knit, you use a lot of your skill, patience, imagination, and best of all perseverance, just to turn nothing into something.

Now you have the basics down for how to knit in your life. With the help of this guidebook and a little bit of practice, you are going to be able to make some of the best home-made products of your life including hats, mittens, scarves, and sweaters.

I encourage you to keep learning about the wonderful world of knitting. This electronic reading material was just meant to act as a primer and get you started on your journey. Check out Revelry and the other websites devoted to knitting. There are tons of free knitting patterns that you can find online. There are also awesome tutorials about how to use other materials for knitting (like plastic). You can also learn how to recycle yarn from old clothing and blankets of your own or that you find at thrift stores.

Also, look around for knitting groups in your area. Many meet a few times a month at a church or even at a local yarn store. Oh, and if you get stuck, call up the local yarn shop or stop by. Often, the people who work there are more than willing to help out new knitters

I hope this was able to help you to learn knitting perfectly using simple steps.

Upon successful completion of this, the succeeding step is to start knitting your first project using all of the information that you have just learned.

CPSIA information can be obtained
at www.ICGtesting.com
Printed in the USA
BVHW060044090221
599629BV00001B/6